# MEMORIES OF TIMES GONE BY

A catalogue record for this book is available from the National Library of Australia



Published 2022

ISBN: 978-0-6455595-2-1 (epub)
ISBN: 978-0-6455595-3-8 (paperback)
ISBN: 978-0-6455595-4-5 (hardcover)

Published with the aid of Jumble Publishing and Editing (https://jumblepublishing.com)

# Image Credits

Hannah

Freesias, Hannah's favourite flowers,
by Joan Whitehead

# Memories of Times Gone By

Hannah Entwistle

# Contents

# Hannah's Story

Hannah was born in a small town in Cumbria on February 22nd 1916, the fifth of six children. Her family moved to Lancashire when she was quite young where she lived for much of her life.

An accident when she was young where she hurt her head, caused one eye to become fixed in the inner corner. At school she was teased and bullied because of the squint and so she didn't have a good experience in these early years. When she had an operation to fix the eye in her teens, she lost most of the sight in that eye and ended up wearing glasses for the rest of her life.

In her teen years, Hannah left school and worked in a cotton mill. She worked for long hours in noisy and dusty conditions. She and the others she worked with learned how to read each other's lips so they could chat during the long hours of their employment. Hannah and her friends would go on bike rides around the region when they were not in the mill, and they roamed for miles to explore the north of England.

At 22 years old, Hannah met and married her husband. She fell pregnant very early in the marriage, but the baby did not survive and was stillborn. Her husband, being a cabinet maker, made the tiny coffin for their baby. Later she had two children, a boy and a girl, both of whom she cared for greatly and they thrived.

Hannah had a difficult life in her early marriage as her husband didn't have a well-paid job and was considered disabled due to his own difficulties with sight; however, she was good at managing her home and the family never wanted for anything. When the children were old enough, she went back to work in a cotton mill in Westhoughton, where she worked for quite some time. After that she worked for a local catering business; not as a caterer, she had the job of cleaning the silver cutlery.

Hannah always played at the British Football Pools, a game that the nation often engages in to guess the outcome of the National Football League's weekly games. As luck would have it, she hit the jackpot and won a substantial amount of money. She had always longed for a home of her own and so, with the winnings, she and her husband bought a small single-story house, or bungalow, in Westhoughton. She and her growing family settled in well and lived there for many years.

Both children grew up and married and each lived quite close in the same town, but her daughter married a man with a vision to travel the world, and that daughter and her young family made the decision to relocate to South Africa. As Hannah and her husband had never travelled beyond the borders of their own country, receiving airline tickets from their daughter was quite a thrill. This holiday made a distinct impression on Hannah with visits to places she had never imagined and seeing animals and cultures she had never experienced. She considered it a 'holiday of a lifetime'.

Life was good in Westhoughton and Hannah and her husband lived very well in their little bungalow. Eventually though her daughter and growing family moved to Australia and Hannah took the opportunity to again explore a new land. This was another incredible experience with a vastly different culture and environment which impressed Hannah. It sparked her imagination to her own creative thoughts and became fodder for possibilities that she might not otherwise have had.

Although her son remained in Westhoughton, Hannah and her husband decided to retire to Rhyl, a small seaside town in North Wales. Hannah's sister lived in the next town, and they settled happily there for many years. Sadly, Hannah lost her husband in 1985, but this didn't hold Hannah back for too long and she gained a new lease of life engaged in the social life of family and friends for many years.

Of course, she made further trips to Australia. She was eager to attend the weddings of both grandson and granddaughter and they very nicely timed their special days so that their grandmother could attend both. She was brave for travelling across the world on her own and did so more than once. Hannah was able to spend time with her great grandson on one visit, a very special event that none of her family will forget.

Hannah spent many more years engaged in the seaside life and times of her small North

Wales home, reading avidly and engaging with her creative craft of writing before her death at the age of 93.

Joan Whitehead
Denmark, Western Australia

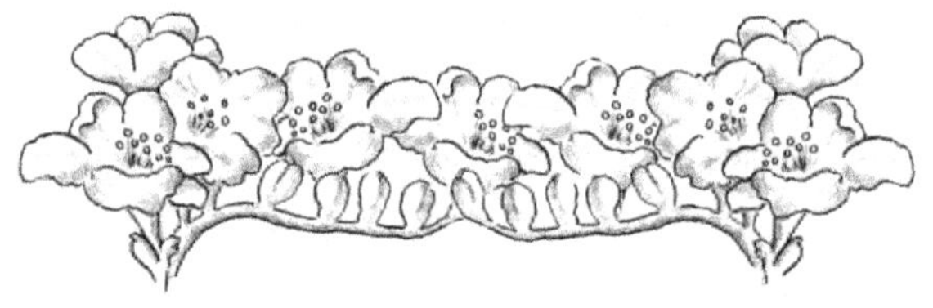

# Poems

## Sunny Rhyl

Come spend your holidays in pleasant, sunny Rhyl
If it's variety you want Rhyl is sure to fill the bill
There is such a lot to do, all sorts going on
Lovely shops, amusement arcades, bowling greens on the prom
If visiting beauty spots is your pleasure, there are lots of them nearby.

Make Rhyl your base, do come and give it a try
The gateway to the mountains, with lovely scenic scenery
Lovely parks well worth a visit, full of healthy greenery
Miles of golden, clean sands where kiddies love to play
Washed by the Irish Sea, always twice a day

If the sun decides to hide behind a cloud of grey
Rhyl's Suncentre will fill all needs till the sun returns to stay
There's theatres and shows where laughter is the aim
Come to sunny Rhyl, you'll be so glad you came.

## Jack Frost

Jack Frost is a busy lad, while we were all in bed
He roams the countryside, no rest for him, he's
working hard instead
He glazes all the windows, a very pretty sight
With feathery swirling patterns, a work of art
alright
He's really in his element, causing havoc
everywhere
If there's a tiny opening, you can bet your life
he's there
He's a very canny fellow, never ever seen
But everybody knows exactly where he's been
Blowing icy blasts everywhere he goes
His specialty is freezing hands and toes
He loves a dripping tap or pool of water there
He soon turns it to ice, he doesn't seem to care
How many unsuspected folk slip and fall head
long
Or how many broken limbs are caused to both
the weak and strong
How many accidents are caused on very icy roads
Or what happens to wild things, animals, birds
or even toads
I suppose it's what we must expect in our wintry,
frosty weather
So please be careful how you go, Jack Frost is oh!
so clever.

## Words

Happy words, angry words, words of praise,
When in the Home League, our voices we raise
We sing, beautiful words, wonderful words of
love.
For our speech we must really thank God up
above,
But how would we feel if we couldn't talk
Couldn't share out thoughts with other folk.
God gave us tongues that we may speak,
Words to cheer others, when life is so bleak,
Comforting words to help someone on their way,
Lovely to hear someone say, "How are you
today?"
Words of love everyone likes to hear,
But some words fill us with dreadful fear.
Words have so many different meanings.
Words said without thought hurt our feelings,
Words said in temper and a friendship is broken,
Those are the words we wish unspoken
But once said we can't ever recall,
Better perhaps not to speak them at all.
We can all hurt or make someone cry
So remember the words "do unto others as you
be done by".

## Problems

People with problems are the disabled and blind
Yet it's amazing how cheerful they are, I find
If your life was spent in a darkened room
No glimmer of light to brighten the gloom
Just think how you'd feel; what if you couldn't
talk
Not able to reply when anyone spoke,
If your thoughts were all trapped inside your
brain.
It's a miracle to me that the deaf and dumb don't
go insane.
Just think how they cope without speech or sight,
Those are the things I would love to put right.
I don't wish to be famous or go to the moon
Or own a big house with an extra room,
If given three wishes and could wave a wand,
My wish to right some of the things nature has
got wrong.

## Taxes

To say we don't pay taxes on our pensions is
tommyrot,
Everyone pays taxes whether they like to or not.
Those dreadful standing charges on gas,
electricity and phone,
We pay a tax before we use them, a unit, or dial a
tone.
Also VAT on nearly everything we need.
There are few things the taxman doesn't try to
bleed.
Now, to confuse us even more and to please the
Euro lot,
Do we have to lose the currency we've already
got?
Do we need to do everything they say? Why must
<u>we</u> conform?
Soon we won't need No. 10; Brussels will be
more like home.
Will someone please enlighten us about just
what's going on?
And tell us, in simple English, to which country
do we really belong.
We sing Britons never never shall be slaves.
According to recent events we're turning into
knaves.

## Voting

Political conferences are with us again
With talk of the Tories' gravy train.
Promises of all sorts of things materialise and
come to nought,
Just as if people's votes can be bought.
But we all know promises are made of pie crust,
So which ever party are we to trust?
The poor and the old are put to the test,
The ones who are well off seem to fare the best.
We'll be courted and coaxed when they want our
vote,
When the time comes we must give it careful
thought.
They all seem to me to be the same,
Yet the political game is a serious game.
Whether it's this party or that who get our vote.
Everyone has their own preference, so politicians
take note.

## Regrets

Oh! My dear I miss you so now I'm alone
Thinking of things for which I must now atone,
Plagued with regrets of things not done.
What dreams we had when we were young,
What ever happened? Other things got in the
way.
We always thought "never mind; there's another
day",
But days go by so quickly and dreams so often
fade
Buried under everyday problems, wishes easily
made,
All too soon opportunity or energy gone.
I like to think we had a good life, when all's said
and done.
Now all I have left are memories of you
And thoughts of things we planned some time to
do.

## Bottles

We had an interesting talk, about bottles, of all things
The speaker had asked us all a bottle to bring
She likened them to people, an intriguing thought
But very feasible, when the imagination is caught.
A sour, unhappy person, a vinegar bottle you see,
While a large comfortable person, a hot-water bottle could be.
A fidgety person, a pop bottle, up one minute then down in the dumps.
While a bottle of bleach really came up trumps
Clean and fresh a real joy to meet,
But a scent bottle person could be sickly sweet.
An interesting subject, don't you think?
One to peruse on when next you take a drink
A variety of bottles, stood on the table
All shapes and sizes, some with, some without labels.
Vinegar, spices, salad cream and sauce
Lemonade, coffee, milk, pop bottles, of course,
Hot-water bottles, scent bottles, hair cream and shampoo
Even a bleach to clean out the loo.
Some were large bottles, some very small,
Ornamental shapes and some very tall,
Flat ones, rounds ones, and square ones too,
Each with their own specific job to do.
Each of those bottles a work of art,

Someone had to make them at the very start.
Think of the processes they must have gone
 through
Before being taken from the shelf by you,
Filled, corked, labelled and packed,
Put into boxes and carefully stacked,
Each with contents valuable in their own way,
Yet, when empty, just casually thrown away.

## Bureaucracy Gone Mad

Decimal currency has knocked us for six,
Counting in tens puts us all in a fix.
A dozen of anything was good enough for us,
This new-fangled currency's started a heck of a fuss.
Fancy a shilling being only 5 pence,
12 pence make a shilling so where's the sense?
We've lost out somewhere, it doesn't seem quite right,
The good old half-crown's vanished right out of sight.
The changed rules and regulations aren't all for the best,
They certainly put our old brains to the test.
Can't do anything but just toe the line,
Daresay we'll get used to the changes in time.

## Thoughts

Going into town early one morning, thinking as I
walked along,
It struck me what a funny old world this is, to
which we all belong.
Like the birds we go to roost when twilight
comes on the scene,
Then, with a dawn chorus of noise, we wake out
of our dreams.
Cars noisily dash here and there as if not a
moment to spare,
Pedestrians rush along, no time to stand and
stare.
Later, traffic tones down to a steady humming
drone,
Then builds up to a crescendo as people dash for
home.
They peacefully settle down like the birds as
twilight softly falls,
To wake and start over again as daylight once
more calls.

## Looking Back

How pleasant to meet old friends and reminisce
Of bygone days, and of that and this,
Lovely to wander down memory lane,
The world of today doesn't seem quite the same.
Remember how we played in the fields of hay
And how the sun seemed to shine all day.
We didn't have TV or money to burn,
Any money we had we had to earn.
Maybe then we were happier too,
Enjoying simple pleasures and making do.
We learned to value and look after things,
To own something and know the pleasure that
brings,
To have pride in something our very own,
Those were some of things we were shown.
The things that come too easily to you,
You don't always value, an adage that's true.

## Constant Noise

Noise, noise, everywhere,
Screaming children, TV's that blare,
Transistor sets rending the air,
Always noise, does nobody care?
Is peace and quite a thing of the past?
Just to be quieter, is that too much to ask?
Cars, aeroplanes, modern inventions,
Constant noise, I'm sure, wasn't the intention.
The way the youngsters rant and rave,
I think the old are very brave
To live in a country geared for the young,
Help for the aged very grudgingly done.
The young of today think of old age they're
  immune,
But the man with the sickle still calls the tune.
Maybe we have made mistakes in the past,
Are the youth of today making anything to last?

## The State of the World

The world is in a sorry state.
It's awful the tales the papers relate,
Wickedness, badness and distress,
Our biggest enemy is selfishness.
The guiles, the tricks, some people employ,
The worse it is, the more they enjoy.
Goodness is laughed at, treated with scorn,
Looked on as weakness and quite out of form.
Laziness, greed, are the things that pay,
Decent standards don't seem to matter today.
You know, I think, the world has gone made.
When you look around, it really is sad.
Children battered to death, violence and greed,
What a fine legacy to our kids we must leave.
Maybe it's because folks take the easy way,
That crime and badness are winning the day.

## The Festival

The Drama Festival is over, it was a real good
show,
Disappointing in one way, we should have won,
you know.
The group worked very hard, they couldn't have
done better.
Word perfect they were, right down to the last
letter.
"The Trial" so realistic, true to this day and age,
We've seen much worse plays on television's
stage.
Don't be disheartened, *we* thought you *very*
good,
What did that adjudicator want—entertainment
or blood?

## The Haven of Sleep

Sleep is a healer of many ills
A variety of needs it ably fills
A commodity everyone requires
One which an insomniac greatly desires.
It's a sea of solitude and heavenly bliss
A haven of rest weary travellers miss.
Where do our minds go when our bodies sleep?
What kind of bizarre appointments do they keep?
When we enter that hall of hallowed peace
Do our minds go blank, all energy cease?
Or is the mind active in our dreams?
A subconscious act we appear in it seems
A fantasy brought on by events in our day?
Or something we long for, so the experts say,
To drift into a dreamless haven of tranquillity
Then wake, with a feeling of vigour and vitality,
Is a thing we all seek, but many don't find
Yet "they say" that it's there, all just in the mind.

## Election Fever

Of party political broadcasts, we're heartily sick
So confusing wondering which is the best party
to pick.
Promises, promises, all the time
Each one handing out the same old line.
What politicians will do to get out vote
We're very important persons <u>then</u> of course.
We all know promises are made to be broken
At election times, a lot of hot air is spoken
Each part trying their best to discredit the other
Hecklers at meetings causing all sorts of bother.
I suppose each one believes their way is the best
Points of view have to be aired before they're put
to the test.
Be very nice though when it's past-election day,
We'll soon see if the politicians mean what they
say.

## A Cycle Ride on a Lovely Spring Morning

To leisurely cycle along a country lane is a pleasant thing to do
Experts say its exercise and very good for you
It needs a little effort to get from A to B
When achieved, it's worthwhile, cyclists will agree.
On a lovely, fresh, spring morning, it's really quite a treat,
The air like wine, unsullied, if off the motorists' beat.
Hedgerows bursting into life, just shouting to be seen
Clean young shoots so full of life, new leaves just turning green
Mountains in the distance, catch the sun's bright rays,
Snow on top, draped like a shawl, worn in Grandma's day,
Newborn lambs, so frisky, glad to be alive,
Run here and there, give little skips, then back to Mum they dive,
Vegetarians we should be, cruel to kill those sweet young things.
Life has a cruel side to it, that's what progress brings.
We pay the price of progress, few country lanes remain
Where once we used to cycle to a horse's clip-clop refrain

We now get motorways, where cyclists are
forbidden
Far better country lanes, where flowers once
were hidden
Shielded by hedgerows, foxgloves could be seen
Primroses and snowdrops, flanked by fields of
green,
Lots of the lovely old wildflowers now are quite
extinct,
Ponds with reeds and bulrushes growing around
the brink,
Motorists miss these lovely scenes when rushing
to and fro
Their aim to do the journey in the shortest time,
you know.

## Learned at the Knee of Mother

Love is a tender emotion we all feel it some time
or another
It's fostered quite early in life, learned at the knee
of Mother
We experience all kinds of love in our lifetime
Sometimes the heart leads us astray
Friends we have trusted prove false and
heartache the price we must pay.

## Houses

Taking a walk in the country I noticed a sign
"Free House".
It got me thinking how many different places
there are about.
There's a terraced house, very modest, standing
in a row,
Where long ago big families were brought up,
where did they go?
Two up-two down, with a toilet in the back yard,
Mothers hadn't an easy time, they worked jolly
hard.
A high-rise flat in a town, is home to many more
But living in such close proximity must be a
dreadful bore.
Then, a semi was considered a very good detail,
While if one owned a detached house you went
up the living scale.
A picturesque cottage with a thatched roof is
many folks' dream–
But it's how you live, not where you live it would
seem.
No house is a home where there is no love,
Whether a mansion, penthouse, cottage, or the
flat up above.

## The Toys' Christmas Party

"We've been invited to a party," said Dolly to Teddy.
"Be quick, and I'll wait for you to get ready."
Arrayed in fine garments, off they set
To the Dolls' House, where their friends they met.
Golly was there, his black face creased in a grin,
Major on the drums, was creating such a din.
The tin soldiers shuffled along, trying to dance,
While the wooden horse, standing on side, started to prance.
Humpy Dumpty was there, he'd climbed down off the wall.
Red Riding Hood danced with Mr Wolf, she wasn't afraid at all.
Oh! What a gay time they had! Father Christmas came
With a sack full of toys, but what a shame
Dolly fell down and her dress was torn.
She sat down and cried, she looked so forlorn.
Soon her tears turned to smiles, when out of the blue
A glittering fairy said, "This is for you."
She handed Dolly a parcel tied up so neat,
Inside was a dress. Dolly cried, "Oh, isn't it sweet?"
Larry the Lamb bleated, "You must try it on."
While she changed, Kermit the Frog obliged with a song.
The dress was so lovely, a vision in net,

She was so excited, she danced a pirouette.
Sailor Boy jumped up and shouted, "Heave-oh, my hearty!"
Everyone laughed and said, "It's been such a lovely party."

## The Motorist's Prayer

Lord, grant me a steady hand
And watchful eye, that no man
May be hurt when I pass by.
Thou gavest life; I pray no act
Of mine may take away or mar
That act of thine. Shelter those,
Dear Lord, who bear me company
From evil of fire and all calamity.
Teach me to use car for other's needs
Nor miss through love of speed
The beauty of this world, that
Thus I may with joy and
Courtesy go happily Life's way
And reach without mishap
Eternal Day.

## Christmas Time

The bells ring out on Christmas morn
Proclaiming gladly, "Mary's boy child is born."
A stable in Bethlehem, lying on the hay
Was where the Boy Jesus of Nazareth lay.
A pity His birthday, a time of good will to all men
Doesn't bring permanent peace the world over
again.
Yuletide is essentially a children's scene,
Nativity plays and pantos are part of the scheme.
Excited children everywhere with faces aglow
Wait impatiently for Father Christmas to show.
A feeling of comradeship and good will pervades
A shame after Christmas it very soon fades.
Christmas brings to mind glittering tinsel and
crackers that pop,
Lighted Christmas trees with dainty fairies on
top,
Homes decorated with mistletoe and scarlet-
berried holly,
Paper hats and parties where fathers are jolly,
Gay greeting cards dotted here and there,
Robins in the snow and angels kneeling in
prayer,
Families gathered together in a happy bunch,
Partaking of a seasonal traditional lunch,
Carols lustily sung, around a blazing fire,
Drinking everyone's health, before we retire
To a well-earned rest, we go on our way,
The clearing up can wait till Boxing Day.

## Thoughts

Don't you think a thought is a very funny thing?
Everyone has them, and what troubles they
  bring!
You can't stop them, they just pop into your head
While washing up, cleaning, or while lying in
  bed.
Some funny peculiar, some funny ha! ha!
Some not worth repeating, but some oh! la! la!
Really it's funny, for thoughts know no bounds
Don't need aeroplanes to get up off the ground
Distance no object, go anywhere at will
Just like magic, yet you only sit still.
How awful it must be your memory to lose
To have no yesterday isn't what I'd choose
But some thoughts are enough to drive you to
  drink
And the trouble we cause when we don't stop to
  think.

## Noise

"Silence is golden," so says the song
But never ever stays that way very long
Cars rattling by, planes overhead
Thunder one sound most of us dread
Children screaming while playing outside
Yet, when quiet, mothers still can't abide
Wondering what mischief is happening out there,
Don't really know which is hardest to bear.
Transistors blaring those silly pop tunes
Guaranteed to plunge us into instant gloom,
But a knock on the door announcing a friend
Come for a chat saves us going round the bend.
Not <u>all</u> noises grate on our delicate shell-like ear
Some are really quite lovely to hear.
Everyone needs a quiet, peaceful interlude
To collect one's thoughts, a little solitude
Like everything else, too much of anything isn't a
good thing
Moderation seems best a balance to bring.

## A Last Goodbye

Life isn't always as we'd wish it to be
We put on a front for others to see
Everyone must, some time, say farewell
Just when is never easy to tell.
We always think it is far too early
To say goodbye to one we love so dearly,
It's sad to think we'll see them no more
But none of us know what lies in store
God has a plan sketched out for us
When He calls we must go with a minimum of
fuss.
They who go ahead don't want us to be sad
Rather to remember the good times we've had.
Life goes on, we can't always grieve
Time is a healer; that, we have to believe.

## Life

The pace of life is really killing
Every moment we must be filling
Work and worry—strife and care
Rushing here—dashing there
Must do this—can't wait for that
Never time—can't stop to chat.
Slow down! Slow down! Before too late
Soon we'll be at that "Golden Gate"
In a loud voice we'll hear Peter say,
"Give an account of all you've done today."
Think of the rushing and work you have done
Was it worth the struggle for the distance you've
    come?
We shouldn't grumble but be content
Grateful for mercies we've been sent
Think of a parable, here's one you can't beat,
"I grumbled because I had no shoes,
"Till I met a man who had no feet."

## Slimming

Oh! Where is my will power, is it that that I lack?
Wonder whose got it? I must get it back.
Was it stolen or did it just walk away
Disgusted at bulges on display?
I've tried exercising, but that did no good
Makes me feel hungry, and I don't think it
should.
I want to look nice, but it isn't just pride
That makes me want my bulges to hide.
My summer dresses are 38-inch hips
To squeeze in a 40-inch have you got any tips?
No money in purse to go to buy new
So slimming is what I'll just have to do.

## Thank You

Thank you, Mr Cheetham Edmead, for the talk
that you gave
The story you told of the people so brave
All the suffering and pain everyone had to bear
The hopes and fears, then finally despair
As friends one by one lost the battle to live
Heartbreaking thoughts those memories must
give
You touched our hearts by your epic tale of the
sea
Apologies, please, for the inadequate vote of
thanks from me.

*Note: John Cheethman Edmead was Third Steward on the British Merchant Navy vessel, City of Cairo, which was torpedoed and sunk on 6 November 1942 in the South Atlantic, south of St Helena. He was awarded the British Empire Medal (Civil Division) according to the London Gazette of 7 December 1943.*

## Dreams in December 7th 1974-January 6th 1975

The other night to bed I went
Was I really in Africa or was it something I dreamt?
Did I really have a holiday out there?
Or can one have a dream other people can share?
I distinctly remember seeing you all
There are lots of things that I can recall.
Did I really dream about that lovely sun?
The good times we had, all that good fun?
That lovely hot weather, those gorgeous blue skies?
No, I couldn't have dreamt those tearful goodbyes.
In the morning I wake to find out it's true
I did spend a holiday out there with you.
My souvenirs I see, here and there dotted,
An elephant, a crocodile, a dress navy blue-spotted.
Memories flood back of the good times we had
Dreams do come true, things can't all be bad
Memories will last though our suntans fade
Yes, we'll always remember that trip that we made.

## Time

Time never stands till, it ticks mercilessly on
Before we know it, there's another hour gone
Every second counts when you are in a mad rush
That's when Father time gives the clock a push
Making the fingers just whiz by
Oh, dear me, how time does fly!
Old Father Time is a stern taskmaster
When enjoying oneself, he makes time go faster
But try doing something you just hate to do
And time will stand still just to spite you
Each minute that goes by, we'll never recapture
We think we do, when it's recalled a short time after
But minutes can only be lived one at a time
So make each one count, make it really worthwhile
Live life to the full, enjoy those fleeting hours
Don't waste precious time bemoaning the showers
Look for the sunshine which follows the rain
For time marches on, too quick once again.

## Sport

World Cup fever has run its course
The ballyhoo, the shouting and the applause
On their hard-earned laurels may the winners
    rest
And the losers realise they did their best.
The Cup's been presented, the last whistle blown
All the goals scored, the replays been shown.
Next it's the turn of the tennis set
On our screens, Wimbledon-mania is what we'll
    get
Next will be the click of a cricket ball catching the
    bat
And the cry of the bowler shouting, "How's
    that?"
Golf will be the next sport we'll see on our
    screens
Thousands are made out of sport so it seems
It's not just a game played on the green
As Drake bowled on the Hoe, when the Spaniards
    were seen
It's big business, a very serious thing
Players don't battle for the prestige a win can
    bring
Like all entertainers playing on a stage
Glory isn't enough, they still need a wage
The humble pound's not a thing to be spurned
It still has its uses, however it's earned.

## Flying High

You are treated like Royalty up there in the air
All you could wish for, no trouble they spare
You don't need to worry about a thing
Anything you wish an air hostess will bring
The meals are delicious, all served with a smile
As you fly through the air mile after mile
Yes, you fly through the air with the greatest of ease
Nothing too much trouble, their aim is to please
It's really lovely to fly in a VC10
I hope some time we can do it again
You know, dreams really do come true
Mine did, I know, when we visited you.

## A Day's Outing

The weather was beautiful as we took to the road
Through the town and into the countryside we drove
Up winding, steep hills at a crawling pace
Through leafy, sunny passes, which looked like lace
The coach drive, named Harry, kept us all in the picture
A loud-speaker informed us of every interesting feature
Once a beautiful maple tree was shown en route
Even went through a woollen mill, on our day out
The peaceful scene of Lloyd George's grave
The home of Lawrence of Arabia, whose deeds were brave
Peacocks strutting on a castle wall
Were some of the sights enjoyed by all
Dolgarrog once a village of mourning
When a flood drowned many people without any warning
The grandeur of the mountains with their towering peaks
The serenity of lakes, many fathoms deep
When viewing Nature's wonders, what miracles she performs
Small wonder we poor mortals feel insignificant and small
Cascading waterfalls gave pleasurable moments

Peace and tranquillity away from traffic's
torments
These are some of the things we'll recall
When we think of our day out, away from it all.

## The Traffic Jam

A lovely day, and what a commotion
As car follows car in increasing slow motion
Caught in a jam, finally brought to a halt
Then creeping forward, just on the point of revolt
Hot and bothered and sick with frustration
Accidents are caused by relaxed concentration
Tempers are frayed, risks foolishly taken
As drivers try to break out of formation
Gradually, they all get away
To try to enjoy what's left of the day
To feel the sea breezes, oh, so fresh!
And lie on the beach in all sorts of undress
Relax and unwind, release stress ad tension
To enjoy themselves; work, a word no one
mentions
Tired, but happy, they wend their way back
To dirty towns and high-rise blocks of flats
Where smoke pollutes the atmosphere
And estates where old people live in fear
Everyone can't live at the breezy seaside
So summer invasions we must take in our stride.

## A Happy New Year

The bells ring out the old year and greet the new
A Happy New Year is wished for all of you
Good health, happiness, I hope this is one of the best
A vintage year to outshine every one of the rest
We stand on the threshold of a brand new year
Face it with optimism and good cheer
Make a resolution to let nothing get you down
Remember its just as easy to smile as frown
We all have burdens, some more than their share
And many times we think things aren't always fair
But don't let Mr Gloom step in and win the day
Life's really not so bad if viewed the right way
Wipe the slate clean, get rid of all worries and woes
Take one day at a time and just see how it goes
Every one responds more to a cheery smile
So keep your resolution, if only for a while
Who knows we may ever start a brand new fashion
By making this year, the year smiles come off the ration.

## A Cyclist's Lament

The state of Rhyl's roads are a terrible shame
Are the Rhuddlan council the ones who are to
blame?
The stones and glass, the ruts and bumps
Are enough to give any poor cyclist the hump.
Drains, manholes, patches, hazards galore
Bring bad tempers very much to the fore.
It's as bad as riding a cowboy's bucking bronc.
Mind that hole–out of the way–honk! Honk!!
We know cyclists must ride near the kerb for
safety's sake
But do motorists always need all the room they
take?
The majority of motorists are very polite
It's the minority who the give the cyclists a fright.
We know they pay a license and they make it felt,
The arrogant motorist doesn't help.
He pushes the poor rider into the gutter
As he flashes past one can almost hear him
mutter,
"No right to be there, taking up room."
Right from the start, a cyclist is doomed.
The almighty engine is king of the road
Much bigger than us, so can ignore the code.
No wonder accidents happen, it's really no fun
But the state of the roads must answer for some.

## Smile Awhile

Looking around at faces so glum
Are smiles out of fashion, does no one have fun?
The pace of life is so quick these days
Seems no time for fun, but you know it pays.
It lifts up the heart, makes the step a shade
    lighter
When someone smiles, the day seems much
    brighter.
Attitudes alter, because of a smile
The sun seems to shine through, just for a while.
A smile changes the contours of a face
Ad makes the world seem a happier place.
Next time, when out shopping, give it a try
If you smile at someone, they ae sure to reply
And, gaining momentum, so it goes on
A smile is infectious and so easily done.

## A Tonic

Laughter is infectious, it makes one feel better
A load lightener, let's make it a trendsetter.
It's a real tonic, one of which we should all
 partake
Far better than those the doctors very kindly
 make
Every laugh is precious, in this dreary old life
Not enough laughter, and too much trouble and
 strife.
Now, if we all went about with a smile on our
 face
This weary old world would seem a happier
 place.
So come along, you people; what have you got to
 lose?
Give it a try, it's a plea you just can't refuse.
Everyone has something to be happy about
Some need to dig deeper to find it no doubt.
Don't let this old world get you down, keep on
 smiling,
Every cloud, "so they say," has a silver lining.

## Spring

Spring is really coming I think
Crocuses and daffies are on the brink
Of bursting right out of their shell
Spring exuberance nothing can quell
Soon, hundreds of daffs will dance in the breeze
Like a golden carpet spread under the trees
Horrid, cold old winter, just a memory will be
Mother Earth will wake and the flowers will be
    free
Daffodils nodding their lovely trumpety heads
Call all the flowers, "Get up, get out of bed."
Tulips answer the call, they won't be long, I know
Aubretia and forget-me-nots will be the next to
    show
Soon roses will be here in every kind of hue
They really are so lovely, a song of praise is due
To a real old English garden, there's nothing to
    compare
What would the world be like without a garden
    fair
To wander in a garden or just to stand and stare
Beauty is there for everyone, all of us to share.

## The Library

The library holds books of every description
For you to browse through, all worthy of
inspection
Whichever you choose to peruse at your leisure
There are tastes there to suit everyone's pleasure
Educational books containing good advice
Some you wouldn't read, not at any price
But a wide assortment of books are enjoyed by
avid readers
Romances, whodunnits or non-fiction by political
leaders
Some prefer Westerns, with a strong cowboy
flavour
While tales of the sea, other people favour
Autobiographies to wile away lonely hours
Other people's adventures we eagerly devour
What interesting lives other people seem to lead
How humdrum in comparison ours are indeed
We get help with problems however complex
they be
Unbiased advice and all of it given free
Whatever the type we like, the library caters for
all
A book is a friend which is always on call
Travel books give an insight into foreigners' ways
Carnegie we should bless to the end of our days.

## Observations From a Seat in a Café

Watching passers-by going to and fro
Here and there, different ways they all go.
Big people, small people, fat and thin,
Fair people, grey people and some with dark
skin,
Tall people, medium-sized and some quite small,
Others perhaps wishing they weren't there at all,
Old people, young people, toddlers and mums,
Babies in prams, some sucking their thumbs,
Folks carrying shopping bags full to the top,
Pass by in a hurry, no time to stop.
Some enjoy walking, with head high in the air,
While others slouch by as if they don't care,
Some look gay, but a few look sad
As if all the worries of the world they had.
Girls tottering by on heels so high
Follow Lady Fashion, how their feet they must
try.
Smokers with cigarettes, puffing away,
Others chew sweets and bulging cheeks display,
Mums with prams and sweet babes on show,
Takes all sorts to make a world you know.

## Different Loves

There's the love of a man for a woman, sealed
with a loving kiss
It matures in a life-long devotion, blessed by
marital bliss.
There's the love of a woman for her first-born,
her baby, her son
Tender, protective, with a touch of awe, a feeling
of wonder, for a miracle done.
She carries her babe next to her heart, loving him
even before he is born,
The pain she bears is exquisite as from her her
creation is torn.
She watches him grow to manhood, makes little
of the sacrifices made,
Her pleasure is repaid a thousand-fold by her son
making the grade.
She sees his interest in another, jealousy quickly
she smothers,
Giving him up with many a sigh, it's all part of
being a mother.

## A Housewife's Lot

Work and worry, care and strife
Who would have a housewife's life?
Trying to stretch the weekly wage
Gets harder and harder, no wonder we age.
Shopping once was a weekly pleasure,
Now it's all rush, no time left for leisure.
A housewife must be skilled at so many trades,
She's no time to be bored, so much to be made,
Cooking to do, in the kitchen she slaves
Over a hot stove, many prayers silently prayed.
Fevered brows soothed, when a patient is ill,
All just part of a housewife's skill.
Into this she weaves love and care,
Doing the job, and just being there.
Who but a wife or mum would never protest
When various tasks put her wits to the test?
She doesn't go on strike, doesn't down tools,
In housewifery, there aren't any rules.
Patience is needed when the going is rough,
Just to be wanted is reward enough.
No, a housewife's lot is not always a happy one
But we wouldn't change, when all's said and
done.

## The Changing World

Whatever's happening to the world, older people
say,
Things weren't like this, in our younger day,
Tricks the kids get up to, really baffles one,
It shouldn't be allowed, when all is said and
done.
Are grown-ups too lenient, or perhaps half afraid
Of repercussions, or not being obeyed?
What about children being seen but not heard
Victorianism reversed, is that's what's occurred?
Has everyone gone mad? The pendulum's gone
full swing
The greedy, grasping ways of today, unhappiness
will bring
Common sense is called for, it's time to call a halt
Everyone should pull their weight, not say "it's
not my fault".

## Treasure Trove

Without a book to read, whatever would we do
Would be a poor world without them I think,
    don't you?
We were taught when young to treasure a book
From them you derive endless pleasure, even
    learn how to cook.
They give you an insight into days of long ago
Before cars and television took over, you know.
It must be awful not to be able to read
Destinations on buses, menus in cafés where you
    go for a feed
To miss having a giggle at cartoons in the news
To see what politicians spout about when airing
    their views
To miss reading the tags at the January sales
Your child missing out on those fairy tales
Just think how dangerous it could be too
Misreading medical instructions could be a fatal
    thing to do.
Yet there are many children leaving school today
Who can't read or write the statistics say
It's sad the wasted opportunities, chances thrown
    away
Apathy is rife, a common fault today.

## The Art of Reading

Without a book to read, whatever we would do?
Would be a poor world without one, I think,
don't you?
A book is a friend, my teacher used to say,
Treat it well, and with pleasure it will repay
We were taught when young to treasure a book
From them you derive endless pleasure, even
learn how to cook.
You can be transported anywhere at will,
Climb a mountain, yet only sit still.
Gain an insight into days long ago
Before cars and televisions took over, you know.
Travel books reveal the wonders of the world,
Sail the seven seas on a clipper, with sails
unfurled.
Autobiographies are interesting too
Telling of other people's lives, and all they used
to do.
We recall Grandma's generation, talk of "The
Good Old Days",
They weren't very good in lots of ways
Little children working and without enough to
eat,
No schooling at all, and running around in bare
feet.
It must be awful, not to be able to read
Destinations on buses, menus in cafés where you
go for a feed
To miss having a giggle at cartoons in the news

See what politicians spout about while airing
their views
To miss reading the tags at the January sales
Your child missing out on those fairy tales.
Just think how dangerous it could be too
Misreading medical instructions could be a fatal
thing to do
Yet there are many children leaving school today
Who can't read and write statistics say
It's sad the wasted opportunities, chances thrown
away
Apathy is rife, a common fault today.

## Signs of the Times

Vandalism and violence seem the order of the day
When a child is too young, no one has to pay.
What about the victim, do they have no voice?
Just to take everything, is there no choice?
Parents are lax, many don't seem to care
How their kids grow up, but some blame they should share.
The old and the weak are pushed back to the wall,
Look after the children is most people's call
They are too young to know when mischief is done
They don't understand, folks say, to them it's just fun
Surely they should be taught right and wrong in the home
And when misbehaving be made to atone.
We all have to live side-by-side in this land
Why can't it be pleasant? Who will make them understand?
If parents don't care about their offspring obeying
The law should take a hand, that goes without saying
It's getting to something when kids make the rules
And old folks are scared to come out of their rooms
After a lifetime of work with a master to serve

To live peaceably is what they deserve.
Can parents not see where their children are
    leading?
A nation of criminals are what we are breeding.

## Reflections by the Fire

Just sitting here dreaming by the fire
Thinking of people everyone can admire
Think of the young and their idols of Pop
Footballers and singers the fans have pushed to
    the top.
Seems to me, I must be getting old
That sort of thing leaves me quite cold.
Now the ones who really appeal to me
Are the blind, must be awful not to be able to see,
Must take special courage to carry on regardless,
Courageous and brave I think they must be
People with disabilities who still struggle on
Smiling and cheerful, when even hope's gone
Hiding their heartaches behind a smile
Forgetting the struggle just for a while.
Deafness, too, must be very hard to bear
The only thing we can do is show them we care.
I often think people who always grumble and
    grouse
Are the ones who have <u>least</u> to grumble about.
Somewhere here a moral there must be
We've a lot to be thankful for, don't you agree?

## Bills

Have just received a phone bill and feeling very
blue
I hate to think of days when those dreaded bills
are due
Those crippling standing charges on gas,
electricity and phone
Really make me shudder, I expect I'm not alone.
Does anyone realise the amount we yearly pay
To companies for appliances standing idly there?
£58 plus VAT for phone, before we even dial
£39.60 for gas, that's before we get a trial
Electricity clocks up a mere £39 before the meter
ticks
This amount we owe before one switch goes click
We pay the princely sum of £3.15 every week for
absolutely nothing.
Well! In my book, it's diabolical and shocking
If the price of therms etc were put up we'd pay
only for what we used
And when that awful bill arrived we wouldn't feel
abused
Where did all the promises go of cheap North Sea
gas?
I'm afraid promises are cheap and all are in the
past
So, come on, Maggie, don't let success go to your
head
Spare a thought for us poor old pensioners and
those bills we really dread.

## A Chapter of Accidents

When guests are due and your schedule is tight
Nothing you do seems to go quite right
Cakes sink in the middle, tarts mysteriously burn
Jellies are dithery, not a bit firm
Even the bread cuts up rough
The roast, cooked so carefully, turns out tough
Nervously, you drop things on the floor
And narrowly miss colliding with an open door
You cut your finger then, sporting a plaster,
Try to salvage order out of disaster.
Nearly everything decides to go wrong.
Hubby, irritatingly, hums a tuneless song
Then going to the door when you hear a rat-tat
With trying to hurry, you slip on the mat.
Biggest hurry, least speed, so people say,
You begin to think it's just not your day.
Your visitors are early, you feel a right ninny
Standing there in curlers and pinny
Just when you wanted things to go right
Everyone's dressed up and you look a fright
But you enjoy the laughter and gay repartee
It's really quite nice, having guests round to tea.

## The New Member

The Guild Meeting was in progress and all was
going fine
The minutes had been read and the speaker was
on time
We settled down to enjoy a pleasant hour or two
When a latecomer came in, causing quite a to-do
Mrs Taylor saw her first, but could only sit and
stare
Clutching Mrs Howarth, she pointed to near the
speaker's chair
Hypnotised, we watched as the newcomer sidled
out.
You are wondering, no doubt, what this is all
about
We know we're short of members and people
usually get a greeting
But we draw the line at a small mouse who gate-
crashed our monthly meeting.

## Praises

Let's sing the praises of the gallant few
Who look after the many, they are long overdue.
Nurses in hospitals who don't make a fuss
No job is too hard when they look after us.
Firemen too deserve a special cheer
If needed, we're very glad to see them appear.
Don't let us forget the brave men of the sea,
A lifeboat-man's job looks hazardous to me.
A mention too for those men in blue
Who keep law and order, a difficult thing to do.
The cheery postman we're always glad to see
Especially with good news, if lucky, a premium bond fee.
The little Scouts and Cubs with their Bob-a-Job week
Although sometimes we see them when not quite so meek.
There are lots and lots of people who deserve to be praised,
People who do good in so many different ways.
The good don't need recognition for doing what's right
They don't seek or want to be in the limelight.

## Don't Give Up

When the going is rough and things look black
That's the time to fight right back.
Don't sit down and helplessly sigh
Hoping things will get better by and by.
Give fate a helping hand, find something to do
Take stock of the good things that have happened
to you.
Look around at others, there are lots in a worse
plight.
Don't despair, get up, get on with the fight.
Troubles are lighter if shared with a friend
Who knows just what waits around the next
bend?
Make the best of things, swallow that bitter pill
There are always two sides to every hill
Best to go forward with a smile and a prayer
When the top of the hill's reach, lots of friends
will be there.

## Welcome to the Club

No need to sigh and worry, when reaching
pension age
Retiring isn't hard, in fact, it's all the rage
On reaching 65, you can join the pensioners' club
Some even join at 64 and qualify for a sub
Before you come of age, just write and let "them"
know
They'll send a book for you to sign, then start
giving you dough
You can then look forward to your pension, and
everyone agrees
Over the years, quite painlessly, we all have paid
the fees
It's really very easy, and nice in lots of ways
Course, it has its drawbacks too, everybody says
A right good welcome waits for you, when first
you come along
Don't be shy, it's not so bad, joining our happy
throng.

Signed by an Old Ache and Pains member.

## The Woman's Lot

"God rest ye merry, gentlemen," do you think
that's quite fair?
What about us poor women? We do more than
our share
We have to do the shopping, make the Christmas
cake
Stuff the blooming turkey, then there's the mince
pies to bake
That's after we've bought all the presents and
cards
Really at Christmas, we women work mighty
hard.
We cook and clean, decorate the tree
Fill those stockings pinned up with such glee
Next time we sing the carol, we must alter the
name
From "gentlemen" to "people", it might not be
the same
But at least honour will be seen to have been
done
So God rest ye merry, people, that goes for all,
not just for some.

# Jack

Jack's the lad, he's quite a sport
A Jolly Jack tar, with a girl in every port
Of all the many hats he's entitled to wear
Jack-o-Lantern, he spreads a kindly light
Lighting the way for travellers in the night
But the wily Jack Frost is a Jack to avoid
He does lots of damage, many folks he annoys
Jack Sprat is often quoted as an example
When meaty dishes are set forth to sample
One Jack was clumsy when climbing the hill
He tumbled down as he climbed up with Jill
Jack-in-a-Box gives some a big fright
Just a click, he's there, then back out of sight
A friendly fellow is Jack-of-Hearts
But a bit of a lad, when he stole the Queen's tarts
Jack-of-Spades, the knave of the pack,
With clubs, they are the Jacks dyed in black
Jack-of-Diamonds reminds one of a glittering gem
The things that are called a girl's best friend
But Jack-of-All-Trades and master of none
Is a name that applies to almost anyone.

## Money

What is this stuff everyone's talking about?
Something everyone's after, there's no doubt.
Crimes are committed to try to obtain
Piles of the stuff, transported by train.
Children and old folks die for lack of the stuff,
Why is it so important to most of us?
What is this stuff folks strive to possess?
When owning it doesn't guarantee happiness
Best things in life are free, so "they" say
Yet we all need it in our own different Way.
Folks say you don't miss something you've never
  had
But everyone seems to have gone "money mad".

## Decorating

Dolly thought, looking around, this bedroom
needs redecorating
If she did it herself, just think what it would be
saving.
Very reluctantly, Mum agreed to give her a free
hand
But nothing outrageous now, you must
understand.
She started the job, for which, she was sure, she
had a flair,
Arrayed in old jeans and with a scarf over her
hair.
It wouldn't take long, the room was very small,
So in a flurry of energy, she set to scraping the
walls
But before that was finished she was really
pooped,
This decorating lark was harder than it looked.
After a welcome cuppa, undaunted, she carried
on
Helped, no doubt, by the inevitable blaring pop
song.
Next she did all the paint work in a nauseating
yellow colour
The daubs on the floor she hoped the carpet
would cover.
She'd got lots of paper, didn't want to run short,
Mum hadn't seen it, but was sure to like it, she
thought.

It was dark blue with a pattern of yellow and
green
Dolly thought it the nicest wallpaper she'd ever
seen.
The first piece went on as easy as pie, Dolly was
elated,
Could almost hear herself being congratulated
But some of the lengths seemed to take on minds
of their own
And finished up on the floor all tattered and torn.
Some of the pieces she'd cut were found to be
short
So had to be patched up then matched, of course.
One length seemed to dance about in a grotesque
form
And ended wrapped around her neck, all sticky
and warm.
When she came to a corner, the paper just would
not fit
It had looked so easy when Dad had done it.
Decorating just wasn't her forte at all
Next time a professional would have to call.
Standing back to survey the effect, she slipped on
some paste
Knocking over the paste bucket in her clumsy
haste.
Oh, my, what a mess! She slid all over the floor
Crash went the steps into the bedroom door.
She was sticky, fed up, and couldn't wait for it to
be done
Somehow, she'd thought, it would be such good
fun.

The result wasn't as good as she'd expected it to be
One of the lengths was upside down, now she could see
There were quite a few wrinkles, perhaps they wouldn't show.
Well! She'd done her best, and everyone has to learn, you know
She rearranged the furniture and looked around with delight
But somehow there seemed something that wasn't quite right
Was it the colours? Maybe they were too glaring
She'd get used to them but, perhaps, she had been a bit too daring.
Mum wasn't impressed, saying, "Is this what you call being mad?"
Dad's remarks were more to the point, he said, "Good God."

"I can't see these colours being conducive to dreams
To my mind you can't beat the colour of cream
More likely finish up with nightmares instead
Anyway, you won't see them when asleep and in bed.
Can't say it's my style at all but I daresay it suits you
There's just one little thing you've forgotten to do."
After all her hard work, I'm sure you'll understand Dolly's feelings

On looking up, she found, she'd quite forgotten
to do the ceiling.

## Give Thanks

We should all help the disabled, we're repeatedly
told
Give thanks for the many, many, blessings we
hold
God is good, we who are fit say
How would we feel if disabled in any way?
How the disabled keep cheerful is a mystery to
me
For, if I had to join them, I'd be as disgruntled as
could be
Maybe it's right, the ones with the <u>least</u> to
grumble about
Are always the ones who have the loudest shout
So, thank God, for his blessings and help all you
can
Those courageous disabled deserve help down to
the last man
They don't want your pity, don't need it you see
For they are all happy and busy as can be
But some of your cash would help ease their load
a bit
So, go on, give thanks, all you who are fit.

## Budget 1981

Sheriff Thatcher and her conmen have been "at
it" again
Compiling a budget, guaranteed to cause pain.
Royalty, of course, are alright Jack
It's the working mass pleasures that are under
attack
The measures taken by the chancellor have
caused a to-do!
In the house, I believe, there was quite a
hullabaloo
He gives with one hand and takes away with the
other
All in all, he's caused quite a bit of bother
Those paying a mortgage will be better off, that's
true,
But National Insurance will cancel that out when
new contributions are due
The poor old motorist is again in the front line
I doubt if the rises will cause any unemployment
decline
I fancy the reverse will happen, more joining the
dole
Everything will go up, its very bad on the whole
Really no one, only the exchequer, has made a
gain
But as that's the object of the game, we can't very
well complain.

## Surprises

To ask somebody out of the blue
To tell of the greatest surprise that's happened to
you
Don't you think it's a tall order to fulfil?
Just hope I can tell you what fits the bill
In my lifetime many surprises have I had
Like when my daughter announced they were to
emigrate
An unheard of thing, what would be their fate?
Or the time we were told, you'll have to come to
see
Here are the tickets for the flight, so it's a "fait
accompli".
Or the time my husband, who was a very clever
man,
Decided to make a TV, saying if it can be done, I
can.
He was a genius at making all sorts of things, you
see,
But I was very sceptical at his making a TV
I'd never even seen one and thought it can't be
done
Impossible to see things happening miles away
right here in this room
All sorts of things folk brought for him to mend
But never paid a penny he could spend
He sent away for a kit, £4 I remember he paid for
it
£4 was a lot in those days
I could have spent it in lots of better ways.

He was thrilled with the kit, it looked a lot of
rubbish to me
I just couldn't imagine what the end product
would be.
For weeks he fiddled with wires and condensers,
soldering here and there
Till at last he'd worked it out and hadn't any bits
to spare
Once more he'd done the thing he'd set out to do
Surprising me, and proving he could do anything
he set his mind to
Miraculously, it worked, there was the picture of
a man talking in London as plain as could be
A great surprise to me!!
In the 1950s TV wasn't as popular as today
We were the first in our street to acquire one so
lots came to stare
We had a house full of men on Cup Final day,
Bolton versus Blackpool the teams
Our house was fairly bursting at the seams
I got lots of surprises from that man I married a
long time ago
Bless him, he could make almost anything, but
money, you know.

## A Visit to the Doctors'

This is how a visit to the doctors' should be:
Went to the doctors', the surgery was full
Lots of folks are ill, doctors' lives can't be dull
Always on the go, never ever still
Writing out sick notes, doling out the pill
"Come in, Mrs Entwistle, we don't often see you here
"Anything that's wrong with you, we'll put right, never fear
"Now tell me all your troubles, I'll see what I can do
"That's just why I'm here, to do my best for you
"Are you sitting comfortably, then take your time, begin
"Don't leave anything out about why you're feeling ill
"What a distressing ailment, your head full of cotton wool?
"Doesn't seem to belong to you? Let's see what can be done
"How old did you say you were? There now, that's a good old age
"You must allow for things wearing out when you reach that stage
"Take these pills, they should help if instructions are followed to the letter
"But come back again if conditions don't go any better
"It maybe you will want stronger pills to steady you

"Be careful how you go, don't climb whatever
you do
"These pills should help you, I have no doubt
"Will you send the next patient in on your way
out?"
So off to Boots I went, prescription in hand
To join in the pill pushers' merry band.

This is as it really is:
Went to the doctors' was a bit under the weather
Felt really ill, head light as a feather
He took my blood pressure, I nearly hit the
ceiling
Being blown up, not a particularly nice feeling
Light-headedness was put down to old age
It seems when one is old, they just turn the page
Can't really be bothered by us old has-beens
We shouldn't expect anything else, or so it seems
At one time, a doctor was a family friend
Talk, and he'd listen, not like this new trend
Very busy people doctors are we all know
And can't always have their feelings on show
But a bit more caring wouldn't go amiss
Making one feel like a person, not part of a
business
Maybe that's what it is, just a job, feelings are lost
We're all caught up in the rush and at what a
cost.

## Two Women Talking Over the Fence

Eeh, you do look poorly, you poor old thing,
It's being a grandma, the trouble it brings
Our Alice has just had another, you know.
No! I didn't know. Well, it didn't show,
How many is that? You fair lose count,
She'll her have her hands full now, I've no doubt.
This is the eleventh, a right football team
Eeh! That house must be fair bursting at the
seams.
Aye! I keep telling them it's time to call a halt
But she says it's the drink, it's not our Jack's
fault.
Don't know how he can afford to go to the pub
He doesn't work and she's always in the club.
They get the family allowance and the social's
very good
Then he does bits of jobs, but I don't think he
should.
Well, don't you go and get yourself all upset
It's their affair after all, you look after yourself,
pet,
Why don't you come with me some time
To the Women's League? You'll enjoy it, it's fine
You can go for a meal and have a bit of a chat
Or just play cards or do a bit of this or that
You'll know lots of the ladies who go
It will do you good, what are you waiting for?
That woman goes, you know her, she wears a
funny hart.
Oh! You mean Mrs Snook, she is funny at that.

You're not fair, she's shy and very reserved.
I shouldn't have said that, the title isn't deserved.
I'll call for you next time I go and you'll see,
Take your mind off your troubles and it's
    practically free.

## OAP

Don't be put off by the name
Being an OAP isn't a badge of shame
Rather a merit for battling along
It's quite an illustrious crowd to which we belong
It isn't given to everyone to reach old age
We overcame many things to reach this stage
Even when young some folks are old
It's the attitude of the mind, least that's what I'm
told
But never mind the quantity of the years
achieved
The quality is more important, I believe
How we use the time given to us
Helping each other, not making a fuss
Quietly carrying on, at a much slower pace
Hiding many heartaches behind a smiling face
Trying to help each other along life's seamy way
That's the best thing to do day after day
Just doing our best with life's allotted span
Nobody knows what is God's holy plan.

## Memories

Looking around my little room, souvenirs I see
Of holidays I once enjoyed in country or by the sea
Memories of lovely times, I remember happily
Days of sun and laughter, shared with my family
Though they are far away, I need only look around
And memories I hold dear around me all abound
Crocodiles from Africa, given with love I'm sure
Crystal figures shine and twinkle, crystal, oh, so pure
Kangaroos, with fur like silk, sit there silently
Babies in their pouches, nursed so tenderly
Suzanne's plate of cherries, look very tempting too
But you'd break a tooth, no doubt, if you took a bite or two
Next to my little corgi, an elephant with trunk in air
A horse, an owl, a cuddly koala, a Cornish pixie quietly standing there
A lady in Welsh costume, not a bit out of place
Among my motley souvenirs, which cannot be replaced
A picture of a famous windmill hangs upon the wall
A reminder of Australia, a holiday lovely to recall
A tiny bushman, in Welsh Wales, just think of that
Swag bag on his shoulder, corks around his hat

Lovely coloured shells, what memories they
bring back
Of sun and sand, exciting adventures off the
beaten track
Caught in a frightening freak hailstorm, no
shelter near at hand
Under a very small rock, we crouched, shivering
in the sand
Memories are lovely things to have but don't
quite compare
With having your family round about to visit
then and there.

## The Marathon

26,000 people running in the great marathon
    race
All hoping to finish whatever the pace
26 gruelling miles and 385 yards
Each runner showing a number on their cards
People in wheelchairs, fancy costumes too
Age no barrier, what guts, good luck to you
All types of people, all enjoying the fun
Charities gaining much from the great run
Will be stiff joints tomorrow, I think, don't you,
But what an achievement and dedication too
The spirit of the people was lovely to see
Maybe there's hope for mankind, don't you agree
Helping each other along the way
IF ONLY it was like that EVERY DAY.

## Someone's Mother

The woman was old and feeble and grey
Bent with the storm of a winter's day
Out of the classroom like a flock of sheep
Came a group of boys hailing the snow piled
 white and deep
Amid laughter and shouts of glee a battle took
 place
Snowballs flying about at a terrific pace
Till at last came one of the merry troop
The gayest laddie of the group
He paused beside her and whispered low,
"I'll help you across if you wish to go."
He guided the trembling feet along
Proud that his own were firm and strong
Back again to his friends he went
His young heart happy and well content
"She's somebody's mother, boys, you know,
Although she's poor and old and slow
And I hope some fellow will lend a hand
To help my mother, you understand,
If ever she's old and feeble and grey
And I perhaps may be far away."

## The Cat

A crowd stood gazing up at the old oak tree
Clinging precariously, Mrs Jones's cat they could see
His plaintive cries could be heard all around
As if he was pleading with those on the ground
Evans, the fireman, on his day off, came along with a ladder
But his efforts to reach Timmy, only made him climb higher
Each time he raised his hand to reach out
Timmy scratched him, making the poor man shout
Early to the top of the old oak tree
Up and up Timmy went in his mad haste to flee
Just out of reach, snarling and spitting
Poor Evans black and blue with branches he kept hitting
When the branch he was on gave an ominous crack
Evans thought, "Cat or no cat, I'd better get back."
Just then the cat cautiously climbed down, and Evans swore that he grinned
But as he tried to move, he realised he was pinned
Stuck on a branch, not a bit safe at all
While the crown down below waited expectantly for him to fall
Slowly, very gingerly, he made his retreat

Till, thankfully, he felt the ladder there with his feet
When he was finally once more safe on the ground
He roundly cursed the cat who was nowhere to be found
His trousers had a tear in a most conspicuous place
And, with his hands spread out behind, he rushed indoors with a very red face
Black cats aren't always lucky when they cross your path
You ask Fireman Evans and he'll verify that.

## Me

I'm not very clever, at nothing do I excel
Nothing I do, can I do, exceptionally well
At school never ever top of the class
Usually about third, a pretty average lass
Many things can I do, but can't really claim
To have done just any one thing to bring me
fame
Nice to make a mark on the world, before I die
Do other folks feel the same way as I?
Must be awful, just to go without any trace
Nobody know you've been in any one place
However obscure, content I'll have to be
To know, at least, there's only one, ME.

## Treasure Your Memories

What a precious thing is a memory
Sometimes the mind can be fickle, you'll agree
But to lose all the memories of yester year
How unthinkable that must be
To just have a blank where memory was
Must be a dreadful burden to bear
Not to know what's gone before
No memories with friends to share
We must treasure our memories
Like gold in a treasure chest
Each one, to us, has a meaning
Recapturing our youth sometimes is the test
What would we be without memories
Shadows without a past
They are what life is all about
What makes our happiness last.

## The Christmas Festival

The Christmas Festival took place last week, it
    was quite a gay affair
The heads of federation and mayoral dignities
    were there
We caught the coach to Llandudno and were
    whisked merrily along
Joining other townswomen and swelling the
    happy throng
Townswomen converged there, from towns both
    far and near
Representing Christmas in countries about which
    we only hear
Nineteen different countries were represented
    there
Every one acted out with the greatest of care
Choirs sang, their message ring out loud and
    clear
Happiness to everyone and peace in the coming
    year
All peoples everywhere, whatever race or creed,
Celebrate Christmas, a special family time
    indeed.
We represented Switzerland, each of us doing
    our bit
Walking up the hill to church winking torches lit
On the darkened stage, it must have looked real
    nice
Especially when the sleigh appeared complete
    with fairy lights

Going home, we were thrilled to see twinkling
lights out in the bay
The festival was over, we'd had a busy day.

## Men!!

Is there anything as exasperating as a MAN?
He goes out of his way to be as awkward as he can
There's nothing so maddening as a mere male's logic
The blarney he talks—well!! It's just plain magic
Men, so he says, are the dominant sex
Don't try to deny it or his ego you'll vex.
If in doubt about anything, he'll argue the toss
Just to let you know who's still the boss.
He twists everything around till he's in the right
Even makes it sound as if you'd started the fight.
When watching a programme he's not keen on
He'll talk of everything under the sun
But let him be watching his favourite sport
You start to talk and he pulls you up short.
Slave in the kitchen making his favourite meals
Don't expect praise, if he eats them that shows how he feels
But, you know, he is useful in all sorts of ways
He keeps us in work and so shortens our days
No time to be bored with a man around
He says you hide things when they can't be found
But, under his gruff exterior, my man's really a dear
I'd miss him very much if he weren't here
Men can do jobs we can't we know to our cost
Go on, admit it, without them we're lost.

## Ode to a Spud

It's versatile, lovely, and also tastes good
Don't wish to be without it, even if we could
It's filling, economical, and popular too
A universal dish that is simple to do
As much at home in a pie as a casserole dish
Quite the most adaptable thing anyone could
wish
It can be battered, mashed, or it's easy to fry
This versatile veg on which we rely
Eaten with relish or crowned with sauce
Hot or cold, it's delicious, of course
Sometimes crisped and put in a bag
Lots of different flavours can be had
Used as a fill-up for growing girls and boys
Teamed with anything, a dish everyone enjoys
Fried golden brown and coupled with fish
It's quite a famous old English dish
Piped around a roast, it looks very tempting
Slimmers are horrified by a generous helping
It's laughed at, at times, for the way it is formed
But the common, humble spud is not a thing to
be scorned.

## Happy Birthday

Have a happy day, Mrs Lowe,
Birthdays come and birthdays go.
We wish we could stop the years flying by
Cleverer folk than us have given it a try.
Don't regret the years already gone
Time doesn't stop for anyone.
We don't need a special day to remember you
It's just a thing we like to do.
Happy birthday, love.

We love to remember you, don't need a special
    day
But can't let the day go by without saying,
    "Happy birthday".

## December 31st 1987

December 31st a day for reviewing things happy and sad
Looking back over the year to things good and bad
Everyone's year won't be quite the same
Some might recall '87 with feelings of shame
Others might feel it's been one of the best
While some may feel it's been a year of test
The Hungerford killings, unnecessary and bad
The IRA bombings make one feel so sad
The deaths in the terrible underground fiasco
Plane crashes, folks drowning in the ferry disaster
Poor folks starve, while countries wage war
Why don't they learn by what's gone before?
It makes one sad to see how folks carry on
Where has all that lovely Christmas spirit gone?

*Hungerford killings—Michael Ryan (27) shot 16 people (including his own mother) in Hungerford on 19 August 1987 before shooting himself in the head.*

*IRA bombings—Remembrance Day bombing in Enniskellen, County Fermanagh, Northern Ireland on 8 November 1987, resulted in 12 deaths.*

*Underground fiasco—Fire ripped through King's Cross St Pancras underground station on 18 November 1987 resulting in 31 deaths.*

*Plane crashes—take your pick out of Lima, Mexico, Detroit, Michigan (and more!), every month had a plane crash with fatalities.*

*Ferry disaster—MS Herald of Free Enterprise (British) capsized moments after leaving Zeebrugge (Belgium) on 6 March 1987 killing 193 passengers and crew.*

*Countries wage war—another long list which includes Burkina Faso coup, Iran-Iraq war, Eritrean war, Cambodian-Vietnamese war plus wars in Chad, Peru, Sri Lanka, Congo, etc.*

## My First Sunday School Prize

Do other folks keep treasures such as I?
Mementoes of many, many, years gone by
One of mine a book, now tattered and torn
A memory of childhood and the place where I
was born
My first Sunday school prize, received years ago
A picture on the cover, one I've come to know
A thing of no value to anyone but me
But my very own thing, precious, you see
Jesus looks out, compassion and peace on his face
Love in abundance for every creed or race
What memories that book conjures up for me
Tattered and torn though it may be
"The Words of Jesus" is the title on the cover
I carefully turn yellowed pages over
Just a child's book but the message still the same
Is to "Love one another" signed in Jesus' name.

## Memories

A friend and I planned a holiday by the sea
Off we went to Llandudno to see how that would
 be
A hotel on the front was where we planned to
 stay
We can recommend it to anyone if you wish to go
 away
The sun decided that week to go away too
But we weren't bothered there was so much to
 do
A shower each morning then a brisk wall on the
 prom
Back in time for breakfast, a tonic for any one
We climbed the Orme discovering new paths and
 ways
Feeling strained muscles we didn't know we had
 till next day
We even had a jacuzzi one afternoon for fun
The cleanest holiday makers in Llandudno, by
 gum!!
We had fun in the most silly funny ways
Relaxed and happy we were, our worries far
 away
We must have walked miles on our outings out
 there
Nothing compares with a walk in the lovely fresh
 air
There were lots of seats, a godsend to poor
 walkers like us
On going to places inaccessible by bus

We walked and exercised and returned full of
beans
So a holiday without sun does one good it seems.

## Childhood Memories

Children these days don't play games as we used
to do
Hopscotch, top and whip, skipping all the way
home from school
We didn't have expensive ropes, oh, dear me, no!
Orange box rope or Mother's clothesline was
robbed of a yard or so
Remember the chalk marks on the tops as they
spun round and round
Like moving kaleidoscopes there on the ground
Vying with each other as to whose top spun the
longest
The honour going to the one whose whip proved
the strongest
Oh! Those home made whips, a stick and a piece
of string
Carelessly flick your leg, and didn't it sting?
Amazing too, the amount of games one could
play with a ball
I couldn't start to name them for I don't know
them all
I expect, like me, you've run miles with an old
tyre and a stick
Masquerading as a hoop, keeping it straight used
to the trick
It was lots of fun, now hoops seem to have
disappeared
I think we are the lucky ones, maybe we should
feel sad

For today's frustrated youngsters, what
memories will they have?
Vandalism, violence and greed, all quite
commonplace
I'd rather have my childhood memories than the
ones they have to face.

## The Garden

After being away, at her garden Dolly sadly gazed
How fast the weeds grew, she was really amazed
Something definitely would have to be done
But weeding, to her, never seemed very much fun
Arrayed in gloves and armed with spade and hoe
She sallied forth to do battle with the fearsome foe
Some weeds had lovely flowers, a pity to kill them in a way
But before long a heap on the path in profusion lay
She straightened her aching back with a sigh
Promising herself a break and a cuppa bye and bye
The small patch she'd done stood out like a sore thumb
And there was still quite a lot more yet to be done
Scraping together her puny little bundle
She muttered, "There's a lot to be said for a concrete jungle."
She rather envied her neighbours, lazily basking in the sun
Their garden was flagged, maybe that's what she should have done
As she grimly worked on, the thought crossed her mind
Of all the flowers she gave to folks who were kind

Like the crippled lady who lived up the road at
Number 3
How her face lit up, how grateful she seemed to
be
Flowers conveyed a message, so she'd been
taught
And look at the pleasure they always brought
Where there's a will, there's a way, so they say
With a satisfied smile, she put her tools away for
the day.

## Dreams

Musing by the fire, with nothing to do
Thoughts race through my mind, jumping from
cue to cue
If set down on paper, what a jumble they would
seem
Rather like an upside down, crazy, mixed-up
dream
Nice sometimes to indulge in fanciful,
improbable schemes
To dream of life as we think it might perhaps
have been
If fate had decreed a different path for us to
travel
No doubt we'd finish up just the same, but have
different knots to unravel
A dream is like an oasis in the desert of life
A quiet rest by the wayside, from endless trouble
and strife
Of course, we don't really expect them to ever
come true
They are like safety valves, so must be good for
you.

## How Things Used to Be

I sit here for hours, thinking how things used to
be
Can't do much now, can't get about, you see
My thoughts turn to things of the past
When days used to go by ever so fast
I think of the things I used to do
How I wrote verses, read out to you
I sung in the choir, sometimes slightly off key
I'm sure Rita used to sometimes despair of me
But we enjoyed our meetings with Ruth in the
chair
To think I've grown old and can't meet you there
But I have lovely thoughts of the good times we
had
Please accept my best wished, things aren't
always bad
Everyone has ups and downs on life's bumpy
way
Can't always be pleasant so remember the happy
days
With the good Lord's help, we'll all weather the
storms
And eventually reach our heavenly homes.

## Emigrating

Just what can you say when faced with the fact
Your family is emigrating, maybe not coming back?
How do other mothers feel when faced with this news?
How do they manage? What are their views?
I shouldn't try to hold you back, I've had my day
I hope lots of good opportunities come your way
It just does not good to rant and rave
I must hide my feelings, try to act brave
But deep down inside, I can't help being afraid
What's this strange country like? Will they make the grade?
Will they be happy? Are they doing what's right?
Will a prayer help them, if said every night?
I know they are responsible adults, not babies yet
So why don't I stop worrying and getting upset?
I'll wish them Godspeed with a tremulous smile
And try not to think of those thousands of miles
God bless my family, my love goes out there with you.
I hope you find happiness, and your problems are few.

## Music

Music hath charms to soothe the savage breast
But some of the rubbish played today puts nerves to a test
Have you thought there's a tune to suit every situation?
You could have some laughs if you gave it a bit of concentration.
How about singing "My Old Man's a Dustman" while cleaning the grate?
Maybe "Water Music" helps washing in the machine gyrate?
Perhaps we could sing "Get Out and Get Under" while making the bed
Or maybe "Dreams Dreams" would be more appropriate instead.
Aggravating to hear "Rainbow Round My Shoulder" while sloshing through the rain
"Singing in the Rain" would be a more accurate refrain.
"Mud Glorious Mud" would suit many of our by-ways
Those shortcuts we take to cleaner tarmacked highways.
Ironic to hear "Time on My Hands" when rushing around
A faster tempo might help feet move sharper off the ground.
Would you sing "These Boots Are Made for Walking" after missing the bus?

Maybe "Here's to the Next Time" would fit the
occasion for us.
One oldy is true, you'll all agree with me
"Home Sweet Home" is still the best place to be.

## Sitting Here Alone

I often wonder as I sit here alone
Family far away and partner long gone
When we were young and fancy free
If into the future we could see
Would we still be as we are today
Or would we have changed things along the way
Perhaps it's a blessing we aren't given second sight
And rely on a divine power to keep things right
One can't help envying the young their energy and go
But time marches on don't we all know
Before they know it our places will change
And they'll be the ones like us, how strange!!

## Looking Back

Looking back is a sign of old age, so they say
But lots of things look better when viewed in this way
When just a young girl, I worked “below stairs” for a short time
The mistress’s mother paid a visit and decided to stay for a while
The spare bedroom being out of use, she commandeered mine
Banished to the kitchen on a camp-bed, for a time it was fine
One night, about 2.30, in the middle of a lovely dream
I woke with a start, blinded by a torch beam
“Burglars,” I thought, “whatever shall I do?”
What would you think if it happened to you?
All sorts of things, flashed through my mind
The poker nearby maybe I could find
It was a policeman wanting to know
How it was he’d found an open door
Not looking his usual self, the master came down
Viewing the hysterics upstairs with a frown
He took charge, not bothering about me
I was banished to the kitchen to make tea
You can imagine it gave me a bit of a fright
Being awakened by a policeman in the middle of the night
Poor man was never allowed to forget but it’s a thing anyone can do
I bet it’s happened many times to you too.

## The Party

Dolly's parent were away for a long weekend
"I'll have a party," she thought, and rang up her friends
"We'll have sandwiches and cake, and I'll make a meat pie."
She'd never made pastry before, but thought, "Now's the time to try."
Little sponge cakes she made, but they didn't do very well
Perhaps she was over-cautious for every one of them fell
Some resembled doughnuts with a hole in the middle
While others were like drop scones cooked on a griddle
Anyway, she filled up the hollows with icing in pink
Optimistically telling herself, "They'll be alright, I think."
Busy fiddling with the icing, she clean forgot the pie
Still in the oven, it was now black and dry
Well, that's no good, anybody could see
Even the dog refused it, when offered it for tea
She slashed her finger while cutting the bread
So gave up and dashed out for a sliced loaf instead
Sandwiches made and arranged artistically on Mum's best plate

Looked very nice but the proof would be in the taste
She'd concocted all sorts of fancy patés and spreads
Then made a tall pyramid of brown and white breads
Filling a bowl with potato crisps, ready salted
Thought, "These at least can't possibly be faulted,"
But, turning sharply, she collided with an open door
Smash! Went the dish and crisps littered the floor
Crunching over the crisps and rubbing her head
This blooming party she was beginning to dread
A lump on her forehead, her finger sporting a plaster
She tried to salvage order out of disaster
Crisps and glass bowl thrown out in the bin
Along with the meat pie, complete with Mum's pie tin
Surely nothing else could go wrong with her day
"Maybe a party wasn't a good idea," she thought, putting the brush away
Then, rushing to answer the door, she slipped on the mat
Her guests didn't expect to be welcomed like that.
On her hands and knees and in curlers and pinny
What a start to her party, she felt a right ninny
And she'd so wanted everything to go right
Her plans had gone wrong, now she looked a sight

Her friends were early, all looking very smart
So she settled them in the lung, with Dad's
    drinks for a start
Then, dashing upstairs in a mad hurry, she didn't
    take care
When removing her curlers and combing her
    hair
A whole bottle of perfume spilled over her dress,
    what a pong!
How they laughed when told all that had gone
    wrong
From a very poor start, the party went with a
    swing
Surprising what cheeriness a few drinks will
    bring
Dad wouldn't be pleased, his drinks cupboard
    was bare
And Mum wouldn't care for the burn in the
    carpet covered by Dad's big chair
Or the deep scratch on the TV she'd tried to erase
The breakages she'd save up for and offer to
    replace
Nobody bothered when Mrs Jones came to
    complain
Whoever heard of a disco with soft music, it
    wouldn't be the same
Anyway they'd all enjoyed themselves, agreeing
    Dolly had done fine
The first party she gave, she'll remember for a
    very long time.

## Mr and Mrs Average

We courted and married a long time ago
Before the start of the Second World War
Our first home, a modest terraced two-up two-down
In the little Westhoughton Lancashire town
Very proud we were of our little place
In the huge black-leaded grate you could see your face.
No hot water of "mod cons" then
But grateful we were for our little den.
No bathroom, but a toilet down the yard
Lots of folks were the same, so we didn't find it hard.
We polished and scrubbed our small, rented house
Very happy we were, myself and my spouse.
10 shillings a week we paid for the rent,
We worked really hard for every penny we spent.
What we couldn't afford, we did without
Collecting things slowly and appreciating the count.
18 months later the stork paid a visit but didn't stay long
A little girl came but tearfully soon she was gone
Then the war came, with gas masks, rations and blackout
Our town was lucky when the bombs were thrown about
Manchester and Liverpool the targets, quite nearby

But lots of partings and heartaches we had
covered by many a sigh
When at last it was over, we two were four,
Lucky we were, a few grey hairs, but nothing
more.
To bring up our children, we worked harder than
ever
To see them healthy and happy was our pleasure
Just like lots of others, Mr and Mrs Average, you
see
We achieved nothing spectacular you'll agree
But 51 years on we were happily still together
And very luck to have lots of happy memories
To look back on with pleasure.

## I Miss You So

Oh! My dear, I miss you so now I'm alone
Thinking of things for which I must atone
Plagued with regrets of things undone
What dreams we had when we were young
Whatever happened—other things got in the way
We always thought, "Never mind, there'll be
  another day."
But days go by so quickly and dreams often fade
Buried under everyday problems, wishes easily
  made
All too soon opportunities and energy gone
But we had a good life when all's said and done
Now all I have are memories of you
And all the things we planned <u>some</u> time to do.

## Alphabet

A stands for the alphabet we torture every week
B for beat or brain, perfection we try to gain but
 efforts are very bleak
C to "come on" to those postmen when they're
 late
D for "damn" when they go past our gate
E for eloquence, there we really pass the grade
F for frequent, 500 letters we have made
G for "get up and go", go-getters we are for sure
H for holy we are not, but our letters are always
 pure
I for ideas, with those we try our best
J for jerry they might be, just to put us to the test
K for kisses we send on paper every week
L for how we long to plant them on a cheek
M for morning or moon, our times are upside
 down
N for never coinciding, you're up when we are
 down
O for overall we manage, with a bit of reckoning
 up
P for putting up with knowing you are far away
 from us
Q for questions I ask in every letter sent
R for replies I wait for, have to be content
S for sometimes the weeks go winging by so fast
T for tedious at times, when we want them to fly
 past
U for unlikely is the word for luck upon the pools

V for very unlucky, they are only there for us
poor fools
W for when will we learn a bit of common sense
X for xtra daft we are, easy stripped of our hard
earned pence
Y for yes, we still yearn for riches even though
we're old
Z for zealously we'd guard it for our family but
it's very unlikely so we're told.

## God Helps

God helps those who help themselves, they say
But that's not right, He helps all of us, every day.
We all have evidence of His loving care
Little coincidences we hear, show his presence
there.
We seem to forget Him when things are going
well
But, when in trouble, He's the one we can always
tell.
Troubles shared are halved we declare
And feel better when our troubles we share.
The troubles of the world are many and lots
man-made
Yet it's on His broad back they are gladly laid.
In trouble or joy, He's thc one we always know
We can turn to Him, and His love will show.
Reminding us of His presence in mysterious
ways
Guiding and loving us all of our days.

## Our Trip

Our trip this year went very well
The weather was lovely, really swell
Anglesey was our destination
Off we went after picking Ruth up from the
 station
Over the Bridge and onto the Isle
Where at Llanfairpwllgwyngyll we stayed for a
 while
Wandering around the lovely store
But only looking, we couldn't do more
Then after the inevitable cuppa off we went again
The scenery was beautiful, green trees and fields
 of grain
On we rode to Holyhead, the ferry boat was
 coming in in style
Then waiting for passengers going to the
 Emerald Isle
We wandered around for places to lunch
Going off in threes or fours or in a bunch
Looking for all the world like little lost sheep
But we didn't find anyone who resembled Bo
 Peep
Then off again on our travels, leaving the port
Past the atomic station and onto the Beaumaris
 resort
Where a pleasant hour was enjoyed by all
It's a lovely place, worth a longer call
It was a happy crowd who arrived home after
 our trip

I'm sure we are all looking forward to our next
welcome flip.

## An Embarrassing Moment

Everyone has an embarrassing moment they can
  recall
One that happened to me I didn't like at all
Now 15 is a very impressionable age you'll agree
That's when that embarrassing moment
  happened to me
As a conscientious Girl Guide, I attended all the
  weekly meetings
At the church school, and after all the usual
  greetings
The Captain said, "It's much too nice to stay
  indoors
We can always do that in winter when it pours."
So splitting into two groups into the yard to play
  rounders we went
Each to their own position to which we were
  sent.
I was fielding by the spiked railing near a side
  road
The ball was sent way over may, I missed it and
  felt a fraud
Encouraged by the players over the railing I
  literally did sail
And sent the ball back into play right over the
  rails
But on getting back over those rails disaster
  struck
The others were shouting and didn't hear my
  cries, just my luck!!

My dress was hooked up on the spikes, what
could I do?
I was really "hanging on" and didn't like it, would
you?
But wriggle as I might I couldn't get loose
I was stuck like a fish on a fisherman's hook
Or like one of those naughty pictures hanging on
a wall
Not a pretty sight at all
There I hung, showing a vast expanse of bare
thigh, my skirt around my waist
Now regulation navy blue bloomers aren't to
everyone's taste
At 15 and just waking to the delights of the
opposite sex
I had my eye on one of the scouts and was I
vexed
When coming towards me, no doubt you can
guess,
Was the lad I was interested in, and on seeing my
distress
Like a good Boy Scout he rushed to do his good
deed, was my face red!!
In fact, I desperately wished to be struck dead
Needless to say, my hero worship came to
nothing at all
I got a lecture on the perils of climbing and felt
quite small
Never could look that lad in the face after that
So any romance in the air went a bit flat.
I also got told off by my mother for tearing my
uniform dress

But, really I was lucky, those spikes could have
put me in a lot worse mess.

## My Front Garden

My front garden was always a bit of a bore
I looked on it as quite a dreadful chore
The grass just one big unruly weed
Not a nice lawn, although I sowed good seed.
The dandelions, although a lovely flower,
Seemed to have a very strange power,
They certainly overpowered the grass
So I decided to spend some of my hard-earned brass.
Keen gardeners will no doubt view with a frown,
The grass dug up and flags laid down.
Now I've done away with that awful chore
I can devote more time to my flowers once more.

## Carry On Just the Same

Listening to our talk of people in a big city
Carrying all their goods in boxes, it seems such a
pity
Our thanks go out to those dedicated folk
Who unstintingly give of their time to help and to
talk
To try to bring order into people's lives
To help unfortunates sort things out and survive
To do what they can without counting the cost
To help make things better for the poor souls
who are lost
In this world of ours we need folks like that
An imperfect world we live in and that's a fact
Bust so it has been since time began
Since the Samaritan helped while others ran
In these enlightened years we live in, it's really a
shame
We don't seem to learn, just regardlessly carry on
just the same.

## A Great Big Spider

Going to bed the other night
An awful thing there met my sight
A great big spider just over my bed
I'd visions of it falling down on my head
I tried to tackle the horrible creature
Didn't want splattered spider as a feature
Of my lovely decorated back bedroom
And didn't want to go in the garage for a broom
I'll swear it grinned at my awesome plight
It was huge, a truly fearsome sight
So coward I fear, that's what I am
I gave the bedroom door a vicious slam
Discretion being the better part of valour, I would retreat
Fancy letting a thing like a spider have one beat!
The morning came and the spider had vanished
From my bedroom I was well and truly banished
Next time to another bed I won't retreat
I'll be sure to have that broom in easy reach
Muss Muffet was right to run away
And live to fight another day.

## Sitting By Myself

I often wonder as I sit by myself
Why I was left here on my own little shelf
There must be a purpose why I am here
But the reason eludes me every time I fear
Am I destined for something quite unknown
Or just here to vegetate all on my own
Till the man with the sickle calls the tune
And calls me to go, in a voice of doom
To give an account of all I have done
Will I reach heaven or maybe be shunned
Have I been good enough to pass to that heavenly
sphere
Maybe I'll just stay in my little hut and refuse to
appear.

## Christmas

Christmas bells ring out to cheer
Celebrating things we all hold dear
The birthday of Mary's boy child
Born in a stable, so meek and mild
Sent to save the world from sin and shame,
The one we all love, Jesus is the name.

## Jingle Bells

Jingle bells, jingle bells, happy Christmas Day
Everyone happy on this His special day
We love to sing, happy to recall
How our blessed savour, Jesus was born
No room at the inn, so in a stable he lay
Quite content and happy there in the hay.

## Singing

You think that I can do it
And I know that you can sing
But putting words to music
Is quite another thing.

## The Christmas Tree

A fairy on the Christmas tree
Children dancing around in glee
Tinsel twinkling in the firelight's glow
We all have something to thank the Lord for
So let's be happy this Christmas day
Celebrate, toss your troubles away
Just for one day, let's be free
And enjoy Christmas, just as it should be.

## Blessed Babe

We love to tell the story of the Blessed Babe
Born in a stable and in a manger laid
How the wise men came from near and far
Guided to the Babe by the light of a star
Kings also came, precious gifts to bring,
Paying homage to the King of Kings.

## Christmas Spirit

Christmas trees with lights aglow
Children playing in the snow
Happiness and love abound
When Christmastime comes around
If the good will would only prevail
Extending to every valley and dale
Christmas spirit all year round
Happiness everywhere would be found.

## Christmas Way

Oh! What a glorious day
When Jesus comes here to stay
To save us all from sin and shame
Bearing our sins and taking the blame
Let us celebrate His special day
In the old traditional Christmas way.

## Christ Was Born

We love to hear the story how Jesus Christ was
born
And celebrate his birthday every Christmas morn
We sing "Jingle bells, jingle bells" "Happy
Christmas Day"
Everyone happy on His special day
Troubles are forgotten, happiness abounds
When Christmastime once more comes around.
We deck trees with shining lights aglow
While children play happily in the snow
If that good will would only persist
Not fade away like morning mist
If Christmas spirit lasted all year round
Happiness everywhere would be found
But sadly life around us quickly revolves
And the Christmas spirit soon dissolves.

## Love

Jesus loves us all, so the bible says
He shows His love in innumerable ways
Even the little birds flying about so free
Are protected by His love or so it seems to me
He sends the rain to help the lovely flowers grow
Without his attention they would surely die I
know
Nothing is too small to be nurtured by his care
We don't need to see him to know that He is
there
He gives us precious sight so that we may see
The glory of His universe, here and way across
the sea
We think he has deserted us when troubles
weigh us down
All we can do is grumble and show the world a
frown
He gives us ears to hear the many songs we sing
Praises to our gracious Lord so joyfully we bring
He gave us feet that we may go to help one
another
Wasn't it Jesus who once said, "Treat each man
as a brother?"
So many things he's given us, if we just look
around
But we are apt to take for granted the good
things that abound
Instead of counting the many blessings one by
one

And thanking Him for all the good things He has
done.

## A Really Lovely Day

Our Christmas party went off rather well
At least as far as I could tell
To have a meal made for one is really quite a treat
Ham and salad, sausage rolls, lots of goodies there to eat
Scones and cakes and trifle too
Cups of tea brought round for you
Very funny asking questions as to who
Had green eyes or wore brown shoes
Who had worked in a hospital or had a pet at home
Who had their own teeth or from Liverpool had come
To get us all talking a very ingenious way
Our thanks go to all who made it a really lovely day.

## Home League

From sunny Rhyl's Home League meetings
To bonnie Scotland's, we send sincere greetings
We hope you have as good a time as we always
do
We sing a hymn, say a prayer, and meet our
friends too
We have many a laugh, we are a happy band
Always ready to lend each other a helping hand
I'm sure that's what God wants us to do
To be happy and a good life too
There is so much trouble in this old world of ours
We don't expect it to be all sunshine and flowers
But if we all kept our own little corners happy
and bright
It would surely spread and put a little of it right
Women have an important part in life to play
To bring up our children to go the right way
That's what the Home League motto tells us to
do
Worship, education, fellowship and service too
We are so very lucky in many, many ways
We should really thank Him all of our days
From our Home League meetings we say
God bless and have a happy day.

## A Cup of Tea

The Home League mottos says, "She looketh well to the ways of the household and eateth not of the bread of idleness" (Proverbs 31, v 27)
My kettle is an essential part of my house so I'm told
Shiny or battered as along as they hold water they're in use
We put the kettle on at the slightest excuse
Don't need any experience to use one at all
Every housewife is proficient, especially when any one calls
In times of stress or happiness out it comes in fine fettle
Don't need an excuse to use my old kettle
So common an item I wonder who thought of them in the first place
But you can't say they don't in every household have a place
At one time a kettle hung on a bar over the fire
A black-leaded iron one to provide whatever hot water you require
Not many houses now boast a singing kettle on the hob
Now they are electric ones that do the same job
In Mother's day we had a copper kettle on a stand
To keep it shining we all, in turn, had to lend a hand
Then we acquired gas cookers, what a thrill!!

My kettle was exchanged for one with a whistle,
ever so shrill
Claiming attention no matter where you go
A whistling kettle you just can't ignore
We even had a special one to use on a picnic
stove
An important part of the outing, no matter
wherever we drove
In all sorts of places my kettle has been
On that primus stove it worked like a dream
For a picnic tea there's nothing to compare
With a cup of tea brewed in the open air
Every household has a kettle to boil water in I'm
sure
A cup of tea a remedy for all ailments, a pleasant
cure
Now I've progressed to a jug kettle, electric and
clean
A wipe with a damp cloth all it needs it would
seem
But it's an essential part of every household,
don't you agree?
I couldn't do without my kettle to make my
precious cup of tea.

## Easter

We celebrate Easter this coming week
Chocolate eggs and simnel cakes we eat
Hot cross buns, symbolic of the cross on which
He was nailed
But looking at the world today His lessons we've
failed
What cruel sharp thorns they placed upon His
head
Yet, "Father, forgive them," is what he said
Looking down from His heavenly throne
Seeing the world today, He must surely groan
Wars and killings still go on, was His sacrifice all
in vain?
All the sufferings, all the terrible pain
"Father, forgive them, they know not what they
do"
Easter's a good time to call a truce I think, don't
you?

## No Room at the Inn

There was a census once long ago
When Mary and Joseph to register had to go
No room at the inn while they waited to fill in the form
So they settled for a stable where Jesus was born
We love to tell the story of the Blessed Babe
Born in a stable and in a manger laid
How the wise men came from near and far
Guided by the light of a shining star
Kings also came, precious gifts to bring
Paying homage to the King of Kings
Yet sadly people are still homeless, people oppressed
Jesus must really be awfully distressed
A pity when so many good things have come to light
That so many people are still in a terrible plight
With all the marvellous inventions man has made
You'd think things would be different in this day and age
But we still have poor people and rich who don't care a fig
Thank goodness some seem to care in the way that He did.

## The Passport

Please won't you answer my anguished plea
And send that passport off to me
It's nearly three months since I applied
I must get my plans all cut and dried
I know you've had troubles and hope they are
past
But the weeks are flying by ever so fast
My Australian grandson's wedding looms near
He's anxiously waiting for his Gran to appear
I would so like to see him tie the knot
The fly in the ointment, the passport I haven't
got
So please won't you answer my anguished plea
And post that important passport to me?

Note from Hannah below this poem:
Sent to the passport office in 1981 strike, it did
the trick
I got my passport double quick.

## Tell Him You Love Him

If with pleasure you are viewing any work a man
  is doing
If you like him or you love him tell him now
Don't withhold your approbation till the parson
  makes oration
And he lies with snowy lilies on his brow
For no matter how you shout it he won't really
  care about it
He won't care how many tears you may have
  shed
If you think some praise is due him, now's the
  time to give it to him
For he cannot read his tombstone when he's
  dead.

## Say Them Now

The flowers you are going to bring to my funeral
Bring them now, for I want to see them
The kind words you have to say about me
Say them now, for I want to hear them.

## The Hair-Do

Dolly sat looking at herself, with a critical look
Why couldn't she look glamorous, like the models
  seen in a book?
She gazed at her mousy hair, twisting it this way
  and that way
Thinking of the works' dance which took place a
  week from today.
She'd always fancied being a blonde, but Dad
  wouldn't agree
Anyway, she'd get some bleach and do it
  tomorrow right after tea.
Mum and Dad always went out, every
  Wednesday,
So she'd do it, and confront them with a "fait
  accompli".
She carefully read all the many instructions
Better do it properly, or there would be ructions.
First, she shampooed the despised mop of hair
Then applied the bleach, with the greatest of
  care.
With her head wrapped in a towel, Arab-style
She mused on her parents' reaction with a
  satisfied smile.
When the time was up, the turban she quickly
  removed
Just couldn't wait to see how her looks had
  improved.
She stared and stared, not believing what she
  had seen

For the thing staring back had hair that was bright green!!
She blinked and looked away, it must be a trick of the light
But on looking again, saw it was still there alright.
The Incredible Hulk and one of the Muppets rolled into one
Oh, good heavens! What had she done wrong?
She tried different shampoos, rubbing till her head was sore
But it just brought the nasty green colour up more.
She wished now she hadn't had this blooming fad
Even mousy hair was better than this colour she had.
She couldn't face her workmates, she'd never live this down
Best visit a hairdresser, one preferably from the next town.
She knew what to expect from her Dad, never fear
Mum took one look and promptly burst into tears.
Dad went on and on about daft things she had done
Anyone would think she'd done this just for fun.
"I can't go to work tomorrow," she wailed, "whatever I do."
"Oh, yes! You will," he shouted. "Let it be a lesson to you,

"If you <u>will</u> have these fads, you must pay the price
"Shouldn't meddle with nature, that's my advice."
He relented, of course, and off she went in a miserable mood
The awful green hair out of sight under a thick woollen snood.
The hairdresser surveyed with a smile this spectacle in green
While the assistants gazed in awe at a sight they'd never before seen!
They crowded round, helpfully offering advice on what best to do
Dolly sat there, green hair and her face a distinct reddish hue.
That colour defied all their many skills, it was there to stay
They had to dye it black and cover it that way.
So, instead of a dazzling blonde, she was a raven-haired beauty
In future she vowed she'd let nature do her duty
No more would she meddle with any sort of fad
She'd be grateful instead for the hair she still had.

## Idle Hands

Idleness is a national disease today
Something for nothing is what seems to pay
Satan finds some mischief still for idle hands to
do
I'm sure your teacher was always stating this
adage to you
It's also very true of things today, don't you
think?
For work is from what some youngsters today
seem to shrink
"Idle hands, empty minds," my Mum used to say
Some of the mindless doings answer to that
today
Seems no sense at all to vandalise, they are idle
acts
They are plain vindictive and, sadly, accepted
facts
The adage "manners maketh the man" still
works today
The young thing manners outdated and shy away
They think they can't learn from us old folk
A pity they scoff at us when we talk
"You don't know what it's like today
"Things aren't like that any more," they say.

## If Only

"If only" words spoken by everyone every day
They are quite the easiest words to say
"If only" we hadn't said those angry words at all
Words once said we can't ever recall
"If only" we'd known that something was wrong
Maybe we could have helped if we'd gone along
"If only" we had lots of money to give
To help other people to help others to live
"If only" there weren't so many bad things in this
    world of ours
"If only" everything were sunshine and flowers
But maybe that is asking a bit too much
God didn't promise Utopia after all for us
"If only" folks could live peaceably side by side
What a wonderful world it would be in which to
    reside
If only we knew the right words to say
"If only" quite the saddest words spoken today.

## The Garden

To sit in a garden surrounded by lovely flowers
Makes one think it was worth all the back-
breaking hours
You are nearer to God's heart in a garden, I really
believe
The saying is right, there's magic in every little
seed
Nature is wonderful and when God's work is
displayed
Who else but Him could have all the flowers
arrayed
In their clothes of many colours, a wondrous
sight
Just to look at them is a pleasant delight
But sight alone wasn't the end of His scheme
He created lovely scents to add to our dream
For what pleasanter way to pass time away
Than to sit dreaming in a garden on a lovely
summer's day
A gentle breeze in the trees playing a lilting tune
The birds and bees flitting about on a sunny
afternoon
How tranquil it is just to sit and stare
It seems to give us peace just being there.

## Salt of the Earth

"He's the salt of the earth," they say
It means dependable, good, something unique
today
There has to be salt to bring out the best
A meal without salt would have no zest
So just as in life all sorts must have a place
The good and the bad must have a space
Must mix and do our best to make sure
The salt of the earth help the bad to a cure
I'm sure that's what Jesus tried to do
After all, love one another was his message to
you.

## Traveling

To wander the world at one's leisure
With good company is really a pleasure
To see how other folks live and fare
To see places only read about out there
Traveling is an education in itself too
To meet and talk to folk doing the same as you
Visiting families who've had the urge to roam
But it's also nice to arrive back home
To meet old friends, see what's been going on
while away
To settle into familiar routines day by day
Memories to remember with pleasure
Photos to peruse and laugh at at leisure
Sad to leave families behind, but everything
comes to an end
A good thing there's always letters to receive and
send.

## Hope Springs Eternal

Christmas has just gone and a New Year ahead
"Hope springs eternal," so somebody said
High hopes he'd had when he started out first
The first few weeks he'd been looking for work
As the weeks went by his hopes had diminished
It was now months since he had been finished
Oh, God! Why did that the powers that be close
that pit
Putting so many out of work because of it?
Bosses at the top were "all right, Jack"
It was fellows like him who had got the sack
He was sick of the words "sorry, lad, we're not
taking on,
"Don't you know, there's a recession on?"
If anyone should know it was fellows like him.
He was beginning to think hopes of work very
slim
He'd tried his best but it wasn't enough
Life at the bottom was really tough
Maybe, just maybe, the New Year would change
for the better
But a forlorn hope with so many at the end of
their tether.
Surely, things must change, can't keep on the
downward trend
Let's hope the New Year brings hope the
recession will end.

## It Just Wouldn't Do If We All Liked the Same

To choose six favourite tunes is a mammoth task
There are so many to choose from, it's a lot to ask
Of rock and roll and the high brow stuff, I'm not very keen
While most pop music or how it's presented seems really obscene
Tchaikovsky's music is lovely, Strauss's "Blue Danube" too
While "Phantom of the Opera's" haunting theme does something to you
We listen with pleasure to singers like Pavarotti, Nat King Cole and such
Would be any empty world without our radio button to touch
I really envy people who play an instrument, it must be grand
Wouldn't it be terrible if all music in the land was banned?
The orchestras, brass bands, pianos and the like
If all musicians and singers were to go on strike
Hymns of praise we all sing and are glad
We can enjoy our music, whether opera, country and western, or rag.
It just wouldn't do if we all liked the same
Whatever appeals by whatever name
I think God every day for my ears and sight
And also for being able to get about alright.

To lose those senses, all the money the world
wouldn’t compensate
Well, that’s what I think at any rate.

## Youngsters

Sugar butties, one of childhood's treats
Treacle curly whirlies another one you can't beat
Patterns spread on a thick slice of bread
Better for you than crisps when everything's said
We didn't have pots of money to buy sweets
Like children of today, always demanding treats
We valued them when we were lucky to get a few
And only then if Mother thought it was our due
We didn't think we were badly done to
We accepted it, it was just the thing to do
Not like children of today, wanting this and that
Making nuisances of themselves with ball and bat
Mind you, we weren't always plaster saints
But we didn't go around desecrating walls with paint
To amuse themselves today children have lost the knack
Skipping ropes, top and whip, hoops, a thing of the past
I feel sorry for the youngsters of today
When I see them all out at play
I really think on the whole we had a better time
There certainly wasn't as much bickering and petty crime.

## Memories

Do you remember those faraway childhood days
Those happies little ditties we were wont to say?
We don't hear children of today skipping to those
old refrains
Like Mr Foster went to Gloucester in a shower of
rain
Or tripping off to school with, not sweets like
today,
But a paper with sugar and cocoa in, whatever
would kids of today say
Sugar and a stick of rhubarb tasted, oh, so good!
Remember playing hopscotch with a stone or a
piece of wood
Running with an old tyre and a stick
To keep it going used to be the trick
Children don't seem to play like that today
I wonder sometimes if they really know how to
play
The world is now a different place
Our memories take on a nostalgic face
Those days are definitely gone for good
Would you have them back if you could?

## Hands

Hands are something we cannot do without
They show our feelings when waved about
When explaining a point they are very impressive
Some folks use of them are very expressive
We use them in, oh, so many different ways
They reveal our characters, so fortune tellers say
A firm handclaps accompanied by a smile
Maybe a friend come to visit for a while
A willing hand stretched out to help with a heavy
  load
A gesture of good will, help over a rough rocky
  road
The praying hands, what comfort they portray
While nervous twitching hands worries and
  illness display
But the hand we all need at times is a helping
  hand
Some folks won't accept, on principal they stand
Everyone, everywhere, needs one sometimes,
  you know,
And it isn't the end of the world if you show
Your need for a willing, firm, helping hand now
  and then
Given in friendship and love from your fellow
  men.

## New Year

I hope this New Year will be good to you
In lots of ways and things you do
It's time to make a brand new start
A New Year in which to take part
We none of us know just what's in store
Whatever it is we've been spared for
But let's make the best of every day
Whatever it is the gods throw our way
At times the going is hard, we forget to smile
We think we are hard done by for a while
But things could be worse, we eventually find
Especially if we can leave our bad humour far behind
Laughter is infectious, makes people happy and gay
So let's hope 1996 is the year when worries are kept away.

## The Gift of Hearing

It came into my mind one day as I looked around
How we take for granted hearing every little sound
To hear is a God-given bonus and shouldn't be misused
But sometimes it's hard, especially when abused
Some sounds are melodious and a delight to hear
But some grate on the nerves and are to bear, I fear
The raucous quarrelling voices tearing characters to shreds
Folks don't always realise the hurtful things that are said
The continual pop music today's youngsters can't do without
Always turned so high anyone to be heard must shout
Always noise and more noise everywhere
Traffic on the roads, planes in the air
Continuous disturbing noise is a constant curse
We live in such close proximity consideration is a must
But what a lot of pleasure the deaf must lose
I'm sure it's not what any of them would choose
We must be grateful to hear the many beautiful sounds
And try to shut out the distorted ones we hear all around.

## Bring Something You've Made

When Ruth said, "Bring something you've
made," my brain I had to rack
I used to be quite good at making things, now
I've lost the knack
Used to knit and sew, but not I'm on my own
It isn't worth the cost and effort just for me alone
Sometimes I make the effort to bake this or that
But have to eat it all myself and that just makes
me fat
Some folks are very clear but me I'm just plain
numb
Couldn't do a painting like some folks have done
Doing paintings or drawing just leaves me cold
Can't draw two straight lines, least that's what
I've been told
I like to do a crossword, don't always get it right
But maybe that's because I'm not really very
bright
No Brain of Britain am I, don't even claim to be
Just try to keep the old brain active as can be
If everyone was the same what a dull old world it
would be
And I'm sure that somewhere there are lots of
folk like me.

## Old Age

Is it wrong to live more than the allotted time?
If it is, lots of pensioners have committed that crime
Everything nowadays geared for the young
We were wanted when we were young and strong
The authorities would dearly love to sweep us under the mat
But maybe we are too numerous for that
We brought up our families and paid our dues
Now we seem to be outdated news
We've outlived our usefulness, easy to see
<u>Except</u> when our vote is wanted, don't you agree?
<u>Then</u> we'll be needed and coaxed to vote
So pensioners everywhere take note
There are thousands of us, together we'll make a mark
Come on, you old dogs, show you can still bark
We still have our uses even from a wheelchair
There's life in us old uns yet, so don't despair.

## Being a Pensioner Isn't Much Fun

To be a lone pensioner isn't much fun
No spare cash for things to be done
Much as I'd like to say yes to you
It's a thing I just can't afford to do
Although the pension isn't much fun
I'd love a holiday somewhere in the sun
To see my family in Australia I'd love to do
But my expectancy of winning is all up to you
Maybe I've struck the inevitable low
Especially as I've returned the envelope saying
"no".

## Bereavement

Loneliness is an unenviable condition
Too many finds themselves in this unfortunate
position
One half of a couple, cruelly split in two
Together for years, then suddenly there's only
"you"
The meaning of life is torn away
You drag yourself through every day
Wandering aimlessly all the while
Showing the outside world a fixed smile
After the tears have been wiped away
Somehow you face courage to face another day
The heartache isn't an easy thing to bear
Try as we may, it's always there
But no one can grieve all of the time
A light at the end of the tunnel must shine
Maybe someone will come to show us the way
"Take one day at a time" is what people say.

## Many Blessings

Lord, forgive us for not always thanking you
For the help you give and the things you do
We take it for granted, many times we forget to say
Thank you, Lord, for help along life's seamy way
Sometimes only turning to you when the going is hard
When things run smoothly, your presence we are apt to discard
We thank you, Lord, for the sun's warming smile
For friends we travel with along many a weary mile
We have so many blessings to thank you for
Too many to count, but we want you to know
We are very grateful for all that you do
Though not always showing our love for you.

## Spring Flowers

To see the little spring flowers, it's oh! so nice
Hardly little things braving the bitter snow and
ice
Snowdrops, the smaller heralders of spring
What pleasure these small things always bring
Nodding their dainty heads in the bitter winds
They certainly are lovely, hardy, little things
Crocuses in different coloured hues
Daffies are due in springtime too
Surely the bitter winter must soon be done
When the spring flowers deem it's time to come
Their message is, "take heart, we are here"
The skies will soon be blue and clear
Winter has lost its dreadful grip
No more snow and ice on which to slip
When the flowers don their summery array
Surely the spring can't be very far away.

## All is Bustle

What good is life full of care
We have no time to stand and stare
How true those words of life today
All is bustle, can't bear delay
Most of us own labour-saving machines
Time saved, to waste, so it seems
More haste, less speed, it's true
Is rushing about the best thing to do?
Cars on the roads nose to tail
Tempers raised, it just can't fail
Is it habit? Go with the majority
Don't want to be in the minority
It's a marvellous age which we live in
With all the inventions we've been given
To save us time to stand and stare
Yet life <u>still</u> is always full of care.

## Happy Birthday 14-Year-Old

14 years old, what a lovely age to be
The start of adult life, it seems to me
We wish for you, sweet 14 years old,
The best of everything life can unfold.
Now is the time you feel grown-up and gay
Don't despise advice from older folk along the way.
Listen, you can still do your own thing
Just, maybe, good advice happiness could bring
Always listen carefully, experience does count
Don't ever be afraid to ask if ever in doubt
Be true to yourself, don't lower your sights
Respect yourself, stand up for what you think is right.
Remember, we love you, and we want you to know
We're there in the background, that's what families are for
So if ever you're down and feel a bit blue
Here's someone who'd love a chat with you
We wish you Health and Happiness
Success in your own hands
We hope your future life will be Simply Just Grand.

## Reply to an Invitation to Australia 1981

We've booked our tickets, done our sums
Just hope we're ready when the time comes
Found out our passports are up to date
So that's a relief at any rate
Six weeks we've booked for, hope you don't mind
Coming so far for less would be a bit of a bind
Decided to have a last, lovely, crazy fling
Be left with very little, in fact not a thing
But we're sick to death of bad news, strikes and rising costs
So we'll do our own thing, be money well lost
Haven't had a holiday since 1974
So we'll do it in style, be worth waiting for
So, Western Australia had better look out
Panic sets in when these Entys are about
Just hope we make it, get on the right plane
No doubt, on reaching Perth, we'll be "gradely fain"
So get some teabags in, sure to need a cup
Fancy coming 12,000 miles just for a sup.
Isn't it exciting, six weeks in the sun
Seeing our lovely granddaughter and grown-up grandson
We'll all so be pleased to see their Mum and Dad
For some pocket money we're saving like mad.
Christmas 1981 will be extra special to me
I'm so excited, feel like the fairy on the Xmas tree
Lovely to hear that 6KY band, you know we're band fans

So hope one of their concerts is included in your plans
But don't go worrying what to do with us
Be every happy, just, being with you, don't want a fuss
We'll view lovely Perth, maybe see the sea
Loll about in the garden, hope Scruff takes to me
Seeing your home, later back here we can picture you
When you write to tell us of the things that you do.
I've no doubt at all, we'll get plenty said
Won't be enough time between morning and going to bed
I can't really believe it, how about you?
No stopping us when the bit's between our teeth
Distance no object, no height too high to reach
Whether it's Qantas or British Airways, don't mind a bit
We're doing our best to keep well and stay fit
But you can bet your last dollar, we'll have a good try
So get the flags out, we hope to see you bye and bye.

## Our Visit to Australia December 2nd 1981 to January 10th 1982

We came back to that dreadful winter of 1982.
"Come to Australia for Christmas," said she.
"It's lovely out here and we'd love you to see
"How we Aussies live down under,
"You might like to stay, I shouldn't wonder."
So we paid our fare and got all set
At Heathrow to board a great jumbo jet.
There's nothing to it, it's as easy as pie
No worries at all as you fly through the sky.
Touched down at Damascus, Bahrain and Singapore
If you've never been there, you've a great treat in store.
The terminals so clean (not like some places I know)
Have lovely big shops, with duty free goods on show.
Everything went well, according to plan
Soon there were hugs between Joan and her Mam.
Everyone looks so happy and well
Gorgeous weather, super shops with just everything to sell
Folks don't look as harassed as the British housewives
Facing weekly price rises, bad weather and eternal strikes
Muffled up in woollies to try to keep warm

There, the minimum covering is the accepted norm
Houses, so lovely, really spacious and cool
Make one envious, many even have an outdoor swimming pool
Course, everyone there have cars, some even have three
Roads are good, petrol cheap, it's as easy as can be
They have a good life in the sunshine out there
Perth <u>really</u> is "The Beautiful City" as all the posters declare
We visited lots of places, were looked after a treat
Temperature nearing the 100s, that's quite a lot of heat.
Went up 33 floors to the top of the AMP building one day
The view was fantastic, quite took one's breath away
All of the city laid out in a massive panoramic view
A good way to see Perth, and all at one go too
Government House, imposing, with fountains on display
Some joker had added detergent in a prank on New Year's Day
Instead of sparkling clear water, soapsuds bubbled out
Someone's idea to clean up Parliament, no doubt.
We sample the bowling while out there too
Flat green bowling, not as good in my view

It's taken very seriously, they have all the best
gear
But, unlike us, they can play on all around the
year.
We visited "Lake Monger" where the famous
black swans are
I didn't care for the snapping beaks so stayed safe
in the car
We even went to the races, one of Perth's
outstanding shows
And saw the $200,000 race won by just a nose
We went to numerous places, too many to
mention here
Were thrilled the 6KY band was acclaimed "Best
Band of the Year"
Our grandson played solo at one concert, we
listened with such pride
A tear crept down my check which I did my best
to hide.
While paddling in the Indian Ocean, a little way
from Joan's home
We were caught out unawares by a might freak
hailstorm
Huge hailstones as big as golf balls fell!!
They hurt too as down they rained, pell mell
An overhanging rock was the only shelter to be
had
In ordinary circumstances to go under there, I'd
have thought we were made
Never have I seen such a storm, in any stretch of
imagination

That rock, a heaven-sent haven, in an
extraordinary situation
Lying flat out, watching that hail plummeting
down
As usual our sense of humour surfaced, we felt a
couple of clowns
Nervously, we giggled, we must have looked a
sight
Suppose the tide came in, or a crab thought,
"What a tasty bite."
Given safer, more comfortable shelter, we might
have enjoyed the sight
Of nature's growling giants showing their
fearsome might
Undignified, we crawled out, stiff and black and
blue
Such another experience I wouldn't care to go
through.
We stared at that rock, unbelieving, only 18
inches high
Under which two grown women had sheltered
from the peril out of the sky
We really thought the car would have been pitted
by all that hail
But it had withstood the assault, and we've live to
tell the tale
All too soon it seemed, six weeks went flying by
And sad good byes said, we were once more in
the sky
Winging back to trouble, freezing snow, in place
of sun

Burst pipes, ceilings down, forecast more snow
to come
We're well and truly home again, back to the
eternal struggle
Trying to put things right, coping with all the
muddle
It's back to pen and paper now, for news of
family
Still, we have lots of memories to remember so
very happily.

## Coming Home, 1989

*In 1989 coming back to the awful floods at Kinnial Bay, I went for my grandson and granddaughter's weddings.*

In trepidation I boarded that plane
On a trip to Australia once again
This time I was going all alone
The first time I'd gone anywhere on my own
But I flatter myself I did alright
Getting there a bit battered, not merry and bright
I was welcomed with flowers, just like the Queen
On a safari I felt I had been
I'm glad to be here was what I said
Before tumbling wearily into a welcome bed
The first few days I wasn't too good
A bit disorientated, got the jetlag bug
With loving care, I was soon right as rain
Enjoying the company of family again
Of course, Geoffrey's wedding was first on the list
A very special occasion not to be missed
The bride, so lovely, in satin and lace
Walked down the aisle, so full of grace
Preceded by bridesmaids in pink, flowers in their hair
While the groom in white tie and tails waited at the altar there
The service was lovely, give the clergy their due
Bells rang out proclaiming the good news too
Geoffrey and Joanne were Mr and Mrs at last

No turning back, the die had been cast
The reception was held at "The Room with a
View"
A very apt description of the lovely place too
The view from the windows of the seventh floor
Showed a scene I hadn't seen before
A fairy tale scene of glittering lights
The boats on the river, a spectacular sight
A marvellous sunset, colours of red and gold
A sight really beautiful, a joy to behold
There were lots of new experiences for me
So many things to do and to see
Shopping there is an absolute pleasure
Done at one's leisure in such lovely weather
The shops all air conditioned, clean and cool
The assistants so helpful and polite to you
I visited the bowling alley, the ladies made me so
welcome
To knock all ten pins down with one ball the
intention
But the ball, really heavy, has a mind of its own
When some pins are left standing, you can hear
the groans
They take the game seriously, but also have fun
Climbing the league table is the thing to be done
The annual dinner was an interesting affair
Lots of badges and cups were given out there
I had a go at bowling with the family one night
Didn't realise how hard it was, though I went
with all my might
I think listening to the youth orchestra a bit more
in my line

Geoffrey was conducting and getting along fine
One images Christmas with fires, lights and
snow
Somehow it's not the same in sunshine, don't
you know?
But it was a really lovely happy family time
Celebrated in the old traditional lovely style
A decorated tree under which presents stood
A turkey in the oven, it was really good
Trivial Pursuit was one game we played
But, at my ignorance, I was awfully dismayed
Lots of the questions were Australian ones
Of course, that was where the others really shone
Another new experience was for me
Going fishing from Fremantle Quay
Really a thing on which I wasn't bit keen
Sorry for the poor fish I must have been
They were hungry fish and couldn't wait
To eat the fish bits we used for bait
For every time I reeled the line in
I could see just where the fish had been
The bait was gone, so was the fish
So much for our expected supper dish
We finally admitted our defeat
To the fish shop we beat a hasty retreat
And dined in comfort, but great expense,
On fish and chips, the shop dispensed
So much for my one and only fishing spree
I don't think fishing is the thing for me
Another time to the Indian Ocean we went
To walk along the beach and paddle was our
intent

It was lovely in the beautiful warm blue sea
As clean and lovely as it could be
I couldn't help comparing it with Rhyl's dirty
beach
How far away Rhyl seemed, right out of reach
Halfway around the world, quite a long way
And the return journey I must repeat some day
We visited a famous marine park with all kinds
of fish
Cray, sharks, and penguins, every kind you could
wish
Dolphins so docile and intelligent too
Surprising the tricks they are trained to do
Divers on boards placed up ever so tall
The pool from that height must have looked very
small
They did spectacular dives so gracefully carried
out
No wonder at times we were asked not to shout
A barbeque the next thing we were invited to
Ten of us went and we had a right good do
We had lots of fun playing billiards after the meal
But I must admit barbequed meat, to me, has no
appeal.
Another experience was Gillian's girls' night out
She insisted I went but I had lots of doubts
To a nightclub we would merrily go
But not an ordinary club, I'd like you to know,
A male strip club, nevertheless
Men cavorting about in all sorts of undress
Not a place for one of my tender years
It definitely wasn't tender either on the ears

The noise was deafening, the music so blaring
It really was awful and I had thought so daring
So much for experience, it was a complete
washout
One experience I could easily have done without
But at least we all had a bit of fun
It seems in Australia it's what's generally done
At a girls' night out, a sort of last fling
Before getting married and that sort of thing
Another time we went to a lovely theatre in town
To see a show, a circus affair complete with
clowns
"Barnum", a glittering spectacle of circus life
Geoffrey was appearing in it, it really was nice
They are a musical family, so really no wonder
We enjoyed lots of concerts while I was out
yonder
One morning we had a bush fire quite close by
With filthy black smoke filling the sky
A tragedy for farmers who lost many sheep
It showed them on TV piled up in a heap
Another time an earthquake tremor made us
quake
Skyscraper buildings in town were said to shake
Luckily the earthquake itself was far away
But it was a talking point for many a day
Another time a whirlwind went rushing by
Sending papers and loose stuff flying up in the
sky
Gillian's wedding was the next thing in line
Her dress was beautiful, she really looked fine
In all our finger, to the Cathedral we went

The service was lovely, it was quite a big event
"MV Perth" (The Belle of the River) was where
the reception took place
We sailed down the river at a very sedate pace
The scenery was lovely, viewed from the boat
The lights of the town, reflections in the river
were caught
We enjoyed the cruise, especially the bride and
groom
On reaching port, they left to go on honeymoon
Soon it was time for me to board that plane
To leave my family and come home once again
Back to awful weather and distressing views
Of floods, broken sea walls, shown on television
news
How distressing for the people involved
I do hope their troubles will be very speedily
solved.

## The Disastrous Outing

Dolly Drewe worked in a hot, cotton mill
One lovely day, she said, "I'll play truant, I will
"Get on a charabanc, go for a ride.
"I'll go and see the sea at the seaside."
So off she set, chuckling with glee,
At thoughts of her pals, wondering where she could be
She climbed on a coach and paid her fare
Thinking of all she'd do, when she got there,
"I'll go for a paddle, enjoy an ice cream,
"Might go on a donkey, it would be a scream."
The coach stopped at Rhyl, their destination
The driver said, "Six o'clock back, from the coach station."
Off they all went, eager for a sight of the sea
Dolly looked for a "Ladies", but one she could not see
At last, she found one, tucked down a back street
A funny place, she thought, for a "ladies' retreat".
Anyway, in she rushed, banging the door
And dumped her bag down on the tiled floor
But, when the door she tried to open,
She found it stuck, the handle was broken
"This," she thought, "needs careful planning."
Then she heard a voice, and started banging
But try as she might, nobody came
That door wouldn't budge, it was stuck tight to the frame.
She shouted and banged, till she was fair beat
Then she sat on the toilet, and shuffled her feet

Looked in a loo, oh! wouldn't her pals jeer
Better not tell them when she got out of here.
She pushed and she pulled with all her might and main
Sat down to think, then tried once again
Maybe she could pick the lock like "The Saint" on TV
But try as she may, it just wasn't to be
She shouted and cursed till her throat was sore
She banged and she kicked that solid old door
She even tried praying, but that did no good
She didn't really think anyway that it would
Till at last, just as she'd give up all hope,
She heard a voice, and managed to croak,
"I'm in here, oh! please someone let me out,
"I've been stuck here for hours, nobody's heard me shout."
A policeman stood there, the coach driver by his side,
"We heard the row," he said, with a grin a mile wide.
"You're holding everyone up, it's you whose to blame,
"It's time to go back, home once again."
So poor Dolly like a criminal was marched back to the coach
The driver told everyone, he thought it a great joke
Everyone laughed and her shame was complete
When all the kids were heard to repeat,
"Dolly had a day out, caused a to-do,
"Spent it all by herself, locked in a loo."

Poor hungry Dolly, mortified by shame
Vowed never to play truant, ever again.

## Bygone Days

To see how folks lived in our mothers' day
Off we went on our trip down Wigan way.
In holiday mood, we boarded the coach
To dispel for ourselves, the old "Wigan Pier
 hoax".
Life must have been hard in those bygone days
But folks seemed happier in all sorts of ways.
We say how they worked, even what they wore,
Tools that the used, and what they were for.
We saw the pit brow lasses in clogs and shawl,
Wouldn't care to do that dirty job at all.
The men working in the dark with pick and
 spade
The poor old pit ponies never seeing a grass
 blade.
We visited the spinning mill, saw cotton being
 spun
On spindles and cops, ready for weaving to be
 done.
The world's largest working mill engine was on
 show
A marvel of engineering, well worth seeing, you
 know.
We sailed down the canal, on the waterbus, in
 stately style
Even went back to school, entering in disorderly
 single file.
Sitting at small desks brought many memories
 back

Now all it did was make our arthritic knees
crack.
"Jezebels" were what some of our ladies were
called
When the teacher examined our nails, she was
really appalled
To see them adorned with varnish, unheard of
things!!
The cane was in evidence and we all know the
trouble that brings.
Rita was the star pupil, she was very bright,
Poor Alex, a schoolboy with a moustache, that
didn't seem right.
We all had a laugh about bygone days
But thankfully, they've altered in many better
ways.

## The Home League Rally

It was the Home League weekend at the Windsor
Street Hall
Quite a lot turned up and a good time was had by
all
The band played well, as they always do
Making everyone feel like joining in the act too
There's something about a band playing a
rousing song
It seems to get everyone in the mood to sing
along
The songsters were really good, harmonising so
well
The applause to hear their voices clear as a bell
Our little bunch aren't up to their high standard
we know
But we old uns did our bit and were part of the
show
The speakers talked of the love of the Lord
I'm sure we all agreed, all of one accord
Ruth would like us to have memories like the
lady from Leigh
We're all getting on and keep forgetting, you see
Her dialogues were exceptional, lovely to hear
and marvel at
What a marvellous memory she has to remember
all that
What a powerful voice the young girl has but a
real treat
A contrast to the other lady who sang ever so
sweet

Thanks to the hardworking ladies for the lovely
tea
Without them I don't know where we would be
Also a mention must be made of the gorgeous
flower displays
They were lovely and set the scene in all sorts of
ways
To mix with friends, good music, a laugh and a
smile, a perfect blend
The HL rally was a pleasure to attend.

## Lovely Music

Music hath charms, nothing so true
Good music really does something for you
It lifts your spirits when feeling low
Makes you think life's worth living, you know
A Strauss waltz will get you on your feet
Floating around can be such a treat
The Tritsch Tratsch Polka causes some foot
  tapping
While a dreamy violin concerto takes some
  topping
A romantic love song calms the savage breast
While a rousing march puts itchy feet to the test
Lovely music creates so much pleasure
Tapes and records are things to really treasure
To composers and musicians our thanks must go
Would be a poor world without music, you know.

## Baskets

There are all types of baskets for different needs
Moses was placed in one among the reeds
They come in all sizes and shapes
Jesus used one on the shores of the lake
When with three small loaves and three fish he
fed the five thousand there
And still had crumbs left for the birds to share
A basket is an invention of far off olden days
But used now in many different ways
These days the plastic bag has taken its place
But they aren't as good, they can't stand the pace.
Maybe someday someone will start a campaign
To bring back the good old basket again.

*Note: She would be surprised to find that the old basket has come back.*

## Women's World Day of Prayer

We went to the Women's World Day of Prayer
There were lots of women congregating there
What better way to give God our thanks
For all the good things he generously grants
We talked of women in far away places
Women just like us, but with coloured faces
They have problems just the same as we do
With their families and jobs and money worries
too
We are all on a journey, the speaker said
Don't stand still, keep moving instead
Everything changes, they don't stay the same
Changes are made in Jesus's name
Passages from the bible were read out
Done very well of that there's no doubt
Everyone was in very good voice
The hymns we sang were an excellent choice
Afterwards we all enjoyed Welsh cakes and tea
It was St David's Day, don't you see
We came out of church feeling better, I'm sure
Just hoping that peace in the world would really
endure.

## There's Life in Us Old Uns Yet

Listening to talks about the old, are we all
committing a crime?
By daring to live more than the allotted time?
Lots of us are guilty and maybe should be
punished for that
The authorities would dearly love to sweep us all
under the mat,
Things are generally these days geared for the
young
We were wanted when we were young and
strong
We brought up our families and paid our dues
Now we seem to be backdated news
We've outlived our usefulness, easy to see
Except when our vote is wanted, don't you
agree?
Then we'll be needed and coaxed to vote
So pensioners everywhere take careful note
There are thousands of us together, we should
make a mark
So come on, you old dogs, show you can still bark
We still have our uses, even from a wheelchair
There's life in us old uns yet, so don't despair.

## Spring Can't Be Very Far Away

Still snow and frost the weathermen say
Surely now, spring can't be far away
To see the little spring flowers, it's oh! so nice
Hardy little things braving the bitter snow and
ice
Snowdrops, the small heralders of spring
What pleasure those dainty flowers always bring
Nodding their tiny heads in the bitter winds
They certainly are lovely, hardy little things
Crocuses in different coloured hues
Daffies, lovely springtime flowers too
Surely, the bitter winter must soon be done
When the spring flowers deem it's time to come
Their message is take heart, we are here
The skies will soon be blue and clear
When the flowers don their cheery array
Surely spring can't be very far away.

## Things to Grumble About

World Cup matches, what a bore!!
What the heck do they play them for?
Upsetting everyone's programmes on TV
Not everyone wants to watch them, you see
It it's not football or Wimbledon, it's cricket
For sporting fans, it's just the ticket
When normal service is resumed
And all our old favourites are exhumed
We'll find other things to grumble about
It's human nature, I have no doubt
What did we find to do before TV?
We've lost the art of amusing ourselves, don't
  you agree?

## Happy Birthday

November 13$^{th}$ here again, surely that can't be
  true
Doesn't seem 12 months since your last birthday
  was due
But there it is as plain as plain
Another birthday's here again
Lots of happiness is wished for you
May you be happy in whatever you do.

## The Clatter of Clogs

The youngsters today have no incentive
No need to take notice or to be retentive
What has happened to the pattern of life
No wonder wrongdoing and crime are rife
In the streets of my hometown
The clatter of clogs would resound
As the workers wended their way
To mines and mills for another working day
Voices would be heard in a Lancashire tongue
As first one then another joined in the throng
Now there are no mills, no mines, no work to go to
So what have the youth of today got to do
Technology of today doesn't seem to have benefitted much
When it only benefits such and such
With all the discoveries of today life should be grand
But for the ordinary man in the streets, things seem out of hand.

## 80$^{th}$ Birthday

Can I say thanks to all of you
For the lovely flowers, plant, cards and good
wishes too
You really made my birthday very special to me
I was dreading the day coming, you see
So thanks again for making that day
A really happy and special 80$^{th}$ birthday.

## "Ready, Steady, Cook!"

I like to watch the programme "Ready, Steady,
 Cook!"
The chaps produce dishes good to eat and good
 to look
They have no idea of the ingredients or what is
 produced
In the short time allowed after the magic word is
 announced
Twenty short minutes are all that's allowed
To create a dish and please the crowd
Sometimes the ingredients are very daunting too
I don't think I could do it at all, could you?
It's a fair test of cooking skill
Thrown in at the deep end and still
They manage to concoct some marvellous dishes
With seconds to spare and the best of good
 wishes.

## Go Paint the Town Red

Another year gone, don't give in, though we
know it's hard sometimes
To keep our sense of humour in these blooming
awful times
When things go wrong as they very often do
That sense of humour will always pull you
through
While we can still laugh at adversity
There's still hopes of keeping our sanity
So away with blues, go paint the town red
You only have one birthday a year when all's
done and said.

## "Beautiful Wales"

Our trip out this year was really a treat
Good weather, good company, a combination
hard to beat
Our intent to enjoy the day and have a good time
The sun graced us with his presence making
everything fine
We were awed by the grandeur of mountains so
high
Towering above us and seeming to nearly reach
the sky
Beautiful countryside, it defies description
A real tonic, better than any doctor's prescription
I'm sure we all enjoyed it and felt better for the
change
We are so luck to have such beauty with a short
range
It's surely God's country, "Beautiful Wales"
With its forests and mountains, lovely lakes and
dales
Yet we take it for granted, familiarity breeds
contempt
Thanks to our organisers, the trip was worth
every penny we spent.

## One's Individual Taste

A home by a river or sea might be fun
But, what when they overflow as lots have done?
The damage it causes is not fun at all
The heartbreak starts when the waters fall.
Maybe a house on a hill would be best
But what when Mr Wind decides to blow with
zest?
Then there's the problem of climbing that hill
When age catches one up, that hill could kill.
How about being sheltered by a mountain cosy
and warm
Where neither wind or river could do any harm?
But, foundations of mountains have been known
to slip
Your home buried in a landslide can't be a
pleasant trip
Maybe a house sheltered by trees, like in a park
A home like that might be overshadowed and
dark.
What do you think would be really ideal?
Perhaps it's a matter of how one feels
What appears to one, another might hate
I expect it boils down to each one's individual
taste.

## Decorating

Making ready for decorating, a heavy, weary
chore
But very worthwhile, be nicer than before
Taking down curtains, getting things ready
Perched upon the steps, not a bit steady
Moving photographs of friends and families
Views of places, holidays, with happy memories
Shifting furniture, pushing it here and there
Taking down pictures, stacking everywhere
Scraping off old paper, roses on the wall
Memories of former years, new will be better
after all
The smell of clean, fresh paint lingers on the air
How unfamiliar the rooms with walls so very
bare
Scraping and painting and busily matching
The decorator's enthusiasm is certainly catching
Up to now, my role has been to supply constant
cups of tea
A glorified tea boy, that's what's been required of
me
Creating order out of chaos, a housewife's daily
part
Tired and grimy, but on proudly looking round
Quite worth all the effort, least that's what I
found
How nice it will be to fall once again
Into that cosy, boring rut, of which I many times
complain.

## Time Marches On

I wish that we could stop those years flying
hurriedly by
But no doubt cleverer folks than I have given it a
try
Those birthdays pop up whether wanted or not
A pity we can't just cancel or pretend we've
forgot
But even doing that the toll would still tell
So enjoy the celebration after all, we might as
well
But really the years rolling on is no joke
A good thing it's the same for all the folk
Best just to let the years go winging by
Enjoy them, not spoil them with regret and a
sigh
No need to cry and gnash our teeth
Time marches on, that's one thing out of reach
Wonders may come and wonders may go
But time ticks on whether fast or slow.

## Two Very Brave Girls

Two very brave girls are Elsie and Ann
Where they met wasn't quite in the plan
Each going their own different separate way
Won't forget one fateful awful day
When they met on hospital beds of pain
A thing not to be repeated ever again
Nobody knows when going on a trip
Whether it's shopping or an aeroplane flip
What will be the end of the fling
What certain circumstances disaster will bring
But we don't expect to end up in a hospital bed
Not very nice when all's done and said
But those two brave lasses are fighting back
Overcoming the odds, getting down to the task
Of getting back to normal again
After experiences fit to send anyone insane.

## We Are All God's People

How nice to meet our Australian friends, from
way back over there,
Thousands of miles they've flown, many hours in
the air.
We appreciate their mammoth trip, their views
we love to share,
About people in a different land, who show us
that they care,
No matter where we live, whatever race or creed
We all bring our children up and a good life we
try to lead
Why, oh! why, can't nations live in peace
together?
One big happy family, sharing each other's
pleasure
People in other countries don't differ much from
us
They work and play, raise their kids, with a
minimum of fuss
Helped by their belief in God, whatever religion
is their choice
Against all the world's atrocities, we must shout
with one loud voice
Australian or English, Chinese, Dutch or French,
We are all God's people, from Him will come our
strength.

## Bill

Who is this "Bill" everyone talks about?
Someone very important there's little doubt
He must be a person of well known fame
Yet folks get upset at the mention of his name
He puts many folk in a bit of a state
Especially around any special date
Like when the council tax is due
It seems he's only liked by a certain few.
He gets lots of folk in awful trouble
Everyone knows him, he must have a double
He causes rows and goodness knows what
Can't be a nice man, he doesn't care a jot
Yet they sing "My Bill, he's an ordinary bloke"
But a call from him is never much of a joke
We all get to know him, much to our cost
Not at all pleased when he rattles our letter box
But he's one of those things over which we must
rise
For keeping him happy, you don't get a prize.

## An Apron

An apron, a housewife's uniform
Any shape or size seems to conform
Not like the ones we used to wear
Then, they were made to stand wear and tear
Denim ones in the mill were called "fents" but
just the same
Still an apron but with another name
A weaver's uniform clogs and fent
With tools of trade tucked in a belt
A long sacking apron was what we wore
While stoning the steps, a weekly chore
Even in aprons, fashion takes its place
Now we were flimsy nylon ones trimmed with
lace
Some very dainty with frills and bow
Not very practical but just put on for show.

## Politics

Major and Blair are at it again
Constantly repeating the same old refrain
The electorate are getting tired of their silly fads
And the constant bickering between them like naughty little lads
We know they have their plans to report
But surely they must know its costing them votes
No confidence in politics do they inspire
Lots of folk are even starting to inquire
If they really are the ones to lead the way
And get us out of the mess we are in today
Do we need to do everything the Euros say, why must WE conform?
Soon we won't need Number 10, Brussels will seem more like home
Will someone please enlighten us about just what's going on
And tell us in simple English to which country do we really belong?
The next few years will put everyone to the test
That's why we must concentrate on whatever is best
So get on with it, lay your plans straight down the line
And stop this constant bickering all of the time.

## When

When, oh when, will this draw take place?
Been waiting ages for that special date
Every month bingo more tempting offers
But NOTHING HAPPENS, no cash in my coffers
Please won't you hurry things on
I'm impatiently waiting for that to be done
I suppose I've put paid to anything by saying no
So won't be disappointed, "that's life", how
    things go.

## Who Would I Be

Who would I be if I could change and be someone else?
That's a big question, one to be given much thought. Having just had lumbago and spend a week doubled up like Quasimodo, I wouldn't want to be him.
At one time I longed to live on a small island, what peace and tranquillity to let the world, with all its upsets and worries float by.
Maybe that's a defiant attitude.
I don't want to be famous or have lots of money or be like Mrs Thatcher.
But I have a sneaking feeling for the underdogs of the world and admire people who can stand up and give a speech, someone who isn't self-conscious or never gets stuck for words.
But actions speak louder than words.

I wouldn't want to be in the limelight as nothing I've don't gives me that right
Don't want lots of money, don't want fame
Don't want to be an MP and relegate blame
So if I could change, Mother Theresa I'd be
She's my idea of a great lady, you see
Someone whose compassion and love of mankind
Shows in her actions to both the sick and the blind
But as it's impossible to change and it's not to be
I must be content just to be ME!

## New Year

The bells ring out, a New Year is born
Will it really be better than the one that has gone
A new start, but where is hope?
Will 1993 be a year with which we will cope
Hopes of all kinds are in the mind
A much better year we all hope to find
Full employment, hope many people desire
Hope of world peace, a thing all people require
Marvellous things are invented in this day and age
Yet killing and devastation in places still rage
The old and the poor are the ones without hope
The ones who are nearing the end of the rope
Children crying out for warmth and food
While others are pampered, nothing refused
A balance surely is it too much to ask
Why can't boffins of the world unite in this task?
If only a miracle could happen in this New Year
If a saviour appeared to banish all fear
Hope for the world wouldn't be so forlorn
And the New Year bring hope like a babe newly born.

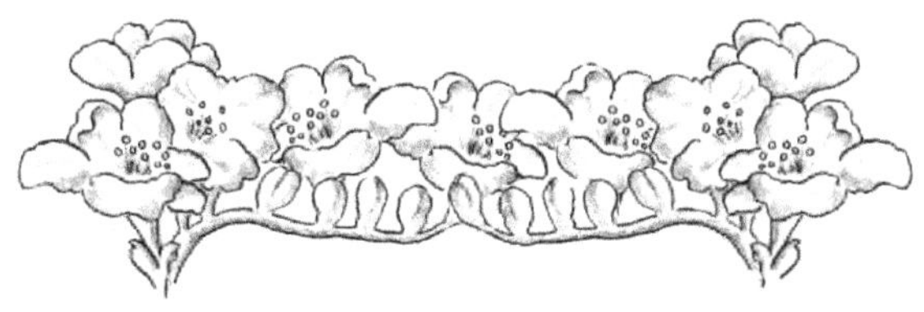

# Stories

## Storm Blacks Out Town

"Hailstones as big as golf balls," read the headlines in a local paper.

1992 came in with a bang for my daughter and I when we were caught unawares by that frightening, freak hailstorm. One minute we were sauntering bare-footed along a lovely, deserted beach in brilliant sunshine, collecting beautifully delicate-coloured sea shells. The next fleeing in the hope of finding some sort of shelter out of the way of those relentless missiles raining down on us.

"Run, put your shoes on your head for protection," Joan cried.

The hailstones rained down on us, hitting their target with unnerving and painful accuracy. I followed her in a blind panic but just where we were running to, I couldn't have said. Sobbing with fright and out of breath, we finally spied one rock with an overhang under which we thankfully crawled. It was all of 18 inches high and normally we wouldn't have dreamed two grown women, one an elderly Gran, could possibly have fitted into such a tiny space.

But this was far from an ordinary occurrence. We crouched there, too exhausted to move; in fact, we couldn't, space was so limited. Incredible how own behaves in desperate unusual circumstances. We were fascinated and terrified but if we could have viewed it from a different, safer vantage point, we may even have enjoyed watching the war of the giants. The elements pitting their mighty strength one against the other, trying to outdo each other's performance.

Hail, such as I've never seen in England, plummeted down, plopping into an angry, wild sea and pitting the sand around with fancy patterns. Thunder growled menacingly and the sky was lit up with jagged flashes of lightning. All sorts of thoughts went through our minds as we crouched in the confined space. Funny, but when in a predicament, bad thoughts are always the dominant ones. We wondered what we would do if the tide came in while we were trapped, or if any of the many crabs we'd seen hiding in crevices, such as we were, decided to join us. Worse still, what if the rock collapsed on top of us? Joan recalled other storms where people had been actually killed by the volume of hailstones; cars with their bodies pitted and wind screens shattered. How was her car faring in a nearby car park?

After seven or eight minutes, the hail changed to torrential rain and we were soaked as it penetrated our inadequate shelter. We were under that rock for the longest 12 minutes of our lives, then as quickly as the storm began it was over and the sun shone again. We crawled out of our cramped hiding place, very undignified, stiff and bedraggled, feeling we'd been in a one-sided fight and with bruises to prove it.

Thankfully, we found the car had fared better than we had and we were quickly on our way home to a much-needed shower and the inevitable cuppa. We soon regained out deflated sense of humour and talked excitedly of our adventure. It was a truly awesome spectacle, and one afternoon of my Australian holiday I, for one, wouldn't forget in a hurry.

I sometimes remind Joan in my weekly letters to give my love to "our rock" when next she visits Burns Beach in Western Australia near the beautiful city of Perth.

# A Holiday

## Friday, March 28th 1993

Off on my travels again. My son took me to Manchester airport, where I boarded a plane at 5.30 for take-off to Singapore. The pilot announced we were to call at Paris to pick up more passengers first. Then began the tedious journey; it seemed endless, about 16 hours. After a lovely meal served by the very pretty Singaporean air hostesses, all dressed alike in colourful long dresses, I settled down to try to sleep, but without success.

Was I glad to reach Singapore, where we had a four-hour wait. The travel agent had put me down for assistance, and I was assisted!! I wasn't even allowed to walk but was pushed from one end of the airport to the other in a wheelchair. I mistakenly thought assistance meant being shown where to go, as I imagined myself getting lost, not having much gumption. At the time, I had a rather hacking cough and they must have thought I had one foot in the grave. I joined a few other assisted passengers in a small room and was given a cup of tea. We all chatted together till we were called to Gate 7 to board the plane for Perth.

Another meal, another film, and another five-hour journey, another wheelchair and off to pick up my luggage. After assuring the attendant I really could walk, I managed to walk through the door and into the arms of my family. I'd never have lived it down if I'd gone through that door in a wheelchair. It was 3.30 am Sunday morning. After a half-hour car journey, I was glad to get into bed, although still feeling I was on the move.

The jet lag passed off after a few lazy days and I soon perked up. To me, the weather was lovely, although I was repeatedly told it was cold, as it was coming up to their winter. The houses are all planned for coolness and have no fires, so we used to sit out in the sun in the mornings to get warm. It was beautiful in the afternoon then cool again at night.

Joan and David had bout a 30-acre block of land at a place down south, a seaside place called Denmark, and we set off to go to view it. It was a three- to four-hour car journey. After leaving the city, we travelled along long straight roads, going through small villages of just a couple of shops, a few houses and a petrol station. No wonder Australians enthuse about our beautiful scenery and mountain passes. We kept a look out in the brush on either side of the road for kangaroos, but all we saw were lots of brightly coloured red and green parrots and cockatoos flying about and a few lizards ran across the road in front of us. It was dark when we finally got to Denmark where booked into a nice motel for the night.

We had to view the block first. I was quite envious; it will be lovely when the house they've planned is built. No near neighbours and a lovely view of the sea. But first they have a lot of work and expense before that happens. The plans include a granny flat, I was told. What a contrast from Perth where everyone seems in a hurry; Denmark is a small place but very beautiful. It has a lovely clean sandy beach where we walked with a lot of surfers riding the waves.

There were quite a few nice beauty spots, but the one that sticks in my mind was "The Valley of the Giants", the giants being the lovely old trees, hundreds of years old, and seeming to stretch up to the sky. They were truly magnificent, mere words can't describe the beauty and peaceful atmosphere there, and walking amongst them one couldn't help but think of being in God's garden. Some of them were hollow after surviving a bush fire; how they kept growing like that I don't know. We all stood inside one of them with lots of room to spare. Lots of photographs were taken and we were awfully disappointed later to find them all spoiled by a fault in the camera. We had lots to talk about on the way home.

Their house was sold while I was there so we had to move into a rented placed till the other one is built; so I was able to help, but constantly being told to stop it. I visited my two grandchildren quite a bit (just a bit down the road, they say, but a full hour's journey away).

We visited another seaside place called Scarborough, but this time only a few kilometres away. I've never seen waves as big. There were a lot of surfers. I would like to try it; it looked dangerous to me.

Another place we visited was Fremantle, a very busy port and shopping area. One shop we went in was like a big fairy grotto with all sorts of fairy-like articles for sale. It was really lovely.

We also had a few meals out, going for Chinese a few times, sampling Chinese cuisine, duck with plum sauce served with rice was one, with Joan and David ably using chopsticks, but I stuck to a knife and fork. We also ate shark with chips, another time we had snapper fish and very nice it all was.

Another place we visited that will stick in my mind for a long time was a ride of three to three-and-a-half hours away, this time up north to the Nambung National Park. We stopped at a place called Cervantes and, not having done enough riding, we booked for a three-hour coach ride to the Pinnacles Desert, going over very rough roads, the lady driver explaining things on the way. She told us they were served out there by the Flying Doctor, they are so far away from a town. She pointed out lots of flowers and bushes growing in the desert and many different species of birds. The desert stretched for miles and dotted all over were the pinnacles, all shapes and sizes, thousands of them, created by the process of wind, rain, limestone, and sand, a natural phenomenon. It was quite awesome and wonderful to see. I can't explain it at all, but I'm glad I saw it. God really does work in a mysterious way. One looked like an Indian chief, another like Queen Victoria and, believe it or not, another definitely had a look of Maggie Thatcher.

It really was an unforgettable experience and one enjoyed by hundreds of people every year, the lady driver said. The heat was terrific and we all enjoyed the refreshing drinks carried in a cool box in the coach on getting back after walking about amongst the weird but wonderful pinnacles. On the way back, she stopped the coach to show us a group of kangaroos standing watching us. David said, "Wave to them, Joan," and she laughingly obliged. What a laugh went up when the kangaroos actually waved back.

Soon, it was time to go to the airport again but the five-hour flight from Perth to Singapore didn't seem quite as long as I had company. Joan and David deciding to come back with me for a few months' holiday. We stayed in Singapore for three days on the way—fancy me in Singapore!! What a place! The heat was terrific on coming out of the air-conditioned airport at well past midnight. We were driven down long tree-lined roads to a huge hotel. Never have I stayed in a place like the "Marina Mandarin" hotel before, a taste of how the other half live. Standing in the foyer and looking up, you could see all the 575 rooms in a semi-circle up to the twenty-third floor. Four glass lifts ran up and down in the centre.

We were on the ninth floor but couldn't resist going up to the top and looking down into the lounge on the ground floor. The tables and chairs looked like doll's furniture. The bedrooms had every thing anyone could want, even a safe to store your valuables. Everywhere was air-conditioned, but going out onto the balcony it was lovely and hot. Our rooms overlooked the large outdoor swimming pool. At night, it was like being in fairy land looking at all the other skyscraper hotels all lit up and the cars on the roads below looking like toy cars.

The hotel had four different restaurants catering for all tastes, a large shopping area and a sports centre with different activities. We were on Raffles Boulevard, only a little way from the famous Raffles Hotel, which we visited later.

One place to go was a must, David said, so off we went in a taxi to see the island of Sentosa. Crossing the harbour in a cable car hundreds of feet in the air, we had a marvellous view of all the ships anchored there–liners, pleasure boats with colourful dragons on the front and lots of houseboats. I thought I'd be scared when I saw the height, but it was a thrilling experience. We went around the island on the monorail, hopping off at different places, then on again. We didn't have time to visit all the places, the Asian Village, Nature Walk, Maritime Museum, etc, etc, but we enjoyed what we managed to see in our limited time there.

Another trip we enjoyed was a tour of the city. It was a pity the market wasn't on that day in China Town, but we saw lots of shops with fancy goods displayed. What a contrast where people lived to the luxurious hotels for tourists. They lived in ugly blocks of flats. We tried to count the number of floors as the bus passed some of them but gave up at 34. We visited a gem factory and saw pictures, ornaments, jewellery, etc, all made of glittering stones. It was really interesting but of course all out of our price range.

An orchid park was another place we visited; it was really something. Lovely flowers in all shades and hues, all growing outside, a beautiful place. A picture gallery was another stop.

We next had a coach trip to Malaysia, queuing at the border to have our passports scrutinised and stamped. The lovely white building, the home of the ambassador, was pointed out to us. It had lovely grounds overlooking the river. Quite a contrast to the typical village house we later visited. We also saw lovely patterns being printed on silk material at one place; very interesting to watch how it was done. Then back to the coach for the stamping procedure at the border again.

I'd have liked a bit more leisurely time in Singapore but as it was soon time to board the plane for the tedious 13-hour flight to Manchester and home. I looked for a glimpse of the Eiffel Tower on approaching Paris but was disappointed. We were served another lovely meal and it wasn't long before the announcement which made us laugh. In a Singaporean accent, the hostess said, "We are now approaching Manchester airport, please fasten your seatbelts."

**Wednesday, June 2nd 1993**

Arriving home, everything looked lovely. My thanks to all who helped make my holiday enjoyable. Now it's back to waiting for the postman for news of my family but I have lots of happy memories of fun and happy times we had together.

Joan and David left Friday, July 2nd 1993, after a great extra holiday. It was lovely having company on the flight too.

## Riding Along

My friend and I travelled many miles together on our bicycles when we were on a lovely holiday, staying with my aunt and uncle at picturesque Kirkby Lonsdale. We shared a big airy attic bedroom which had a view of the river Lune wending its way so peacefully along. One morning, we watched an otter hunt, my sympathies being with the hunted every time. No wonder the Lune is a favourite haunt of fishermen, we spent many pleasant hours watching the water lapping and playfully slapping the boulders under the ancient Devil's Bridge, we meditated on the many stories it could tell if only it could talk. But the river wasn't always so peaceful, its mood changed dramatically to fury after a violent summer thunderstorm. The water rushing along, lashing the rocks in anger, enraged at their immobility and foaming in fury, swiftly taking everything immovable with it. We spent a lovely holiday, alternately sauntering around the quaint old towns of Keswick and Kendal and bowling leisurely along leafy tree-lined country rounds on our cycles.

We picnicked on the side of the road running through the beautiful Honister Pass, the hills making us feel very small and insignificant by their lowering majesty. We visited my Grandma and Grandad's last resting place in the small cemetery near the shores of Lake Windermere, so peaceful and tranquil.

On passing their small white-washed cottage, a vision flashed through my mind of Grandma standing waving to a departing bus.

Riding along in the well-cut plus four trousers Mother had made for us, I could just hear her saying, “Much more decent than those dreadful shorts.” I wondered what Grandma would have said of our mannish mode of attire. No doubt she would have been disgusted at the fashions of the modern miss of the nineteenth century.

The weather was very good to us on that memorable holiday and we returned to work refreshed in body and mind and with a tan the envy of the other girls. The tan would no doubt soon fade in the atmosphere of the stifling weaving shed but we had our memories and were determined to save and maybe repeat it next year.

## Off to South Africa

Can you imagine what thoughts went through my mind when I received a long official looking letter one day, inside which was two plane tickets to South Africa. My husband and I, both pensioners, had been invited for a month's holiday by our daughter and her family, who we hadn't seen for four long years. Never having been on a plane, or out of the country before, we were rather apprehensive but, nothing daunted, we acquired the necessary vaccination papers and passports, and one very cold winter's day in December made our way to Heathrow airport. The flight was absolutely fabulous, everyone being treated like VIPs. We exchanged our bitter cold, frosty weather for lovely, hot brilliant sunshine on arriving after our thirteen hours' flight on a huge VC10 aeroplane.

The sight of our family waiting at Jan Smuts Airport was something I shall never forget, we were hugged and squeezed nearly to death, and all shed quite a few happy tears. They really put themselves out and succeeded in making our stay a memorable one showing us as much of the country as possible. We visited the Golden City of Johannesburg with its huge skyscraper buildings and impressive Strydom Tower, which afforded a marvellous view of all the surrounding countryside. The memory of the jacaranda trees with their masses of beautiful mauve flowers lining the lovely wide clean streets of Pretoria will linger in my memory for a long time. Next we visited the massive stone monument commemorating the struggles and horrors the courageous Voortrekkers endured at the hands of the Zulus before the African colony was founded in the Transvaal in 1838. It really is a splendid spectacle and one I'm very glad to reminisce about any time.

Then on to see the great Vaal and Hartbeespoort dams, their engineering feats were certainly something to marvel at. My small granddaughter and grandson informed us, while going through a town called Vereeniging, that this was the place where peace was signed in 1902 after the Boer War. Fields upon fields of mealies and banana plantations looked unfamiliar to us, the lovely date palm and blue gum trees made colourful photographs, with which we relive our unforgettable holiday over and over again.

Christmas Eve was spent at a large park in Johannesburg called "Wemmer Pan", where we watched the beautiful spectacle of "The Dancing Fountains". Coloured pillars of water rose and fell, and actually danced to the volume of the Christmas carols played. There must have been lots of people there who, like me, couldn't join in the singing because of the lump in their throats, as thoughts turned to absent friends and families. Returning to Kempton Park later in the lovely warm evening, it seems unreal to see the sun glinting on the Christmas decorations in the streets and shops, and fairy lights on Christmas trees in porches of the houses we passed. Christmas Day was spent with friends round the luxurious swimming pool in the lovely grounds of Joan and David's bungalow. Just fancy, swimming in an open-air pool on December 25th, we'll never have another Christmas day to equal that one.

The spacious bungalows out there make one very envious when we view our semis and terraced houses here, there just is no comparison. Not for the South Africans the too close proximity of noisy neighbours, the space there is unbelievable. The shops, so clean, are a veritable Aladdin's cave, selling every conceivable article imaginable, and lots we've never even heard of. We visited a drive-in cinema, a novel experience after television at home. We even watched one day a snake being milked, the venom then used to make snakebite antidotes, a very dangerous but necessary job.

We saw the New Year in at a dance and were entertained by the black waiters playing drums in the traditional African style. New Year's Day was spent in the famous Kruger National Game Park, where we saw animals in their own habitat. Lions, zebra, giraffe, monkeys, elephants and lots more, but my favourite was the dainty little springbok, the national emblem of South Africa, cruel to think of them being food for the larger animals. We also saw a huge baobab tree, and sat under a sausage tree at one of the rest camps while drinking welcome cool Fanta Floats. We travelled along some roads, nearly choked by the dust, saw the awe-inspiring Blyde River Canyon, with its lovely silence one could almost feel, a most satisfying experience, contrasting vastly to the shattering noises of our streets in England. The pull, 2150 metres up the Long Tom Pass, on returning to Kempton Park was really worthwhile, to see the marvellous panoramic views from the top. The weather was a little cooler after a terrific thunderstorm, hailstones as big as peas drumming on the roof.

We visited a gold mine to see the fabulous mine dancers, who were given a great ovation by the crowds who had flocked to see them performing. This was really Africa with a capital "A". Very enjoyable and a complete contrast to TV's "Come Dancing". We acquired a gorgeous suntan and were the envy of all our pale-faced friends when we came home, after saying a sad farewell to our family. Never has a month gone by so quickly.

Back in London, we were approached by a young American who asked if we could explain the problems of our English money to him. It must have seemed as mystifying to him as Rands and Cents had been to us. Immigrants work hard and it would be wrong to give the impression they have no problems, but if our family had they certainly glossed over them. I found myself listening for the chirping of the crickets at night, but was glad we didn't have the nuisance of mosquitoes here. I must have told the story of our marvellous holiday dozens of times, indeed the problem is what not to say as we can't tell all the wonders we saw in our incredible visit. I've even been privileged to speak at our local TWG meeting on my holiday in sunny South Africa, finishing with this verse I sent to my daughter saying our holiday now seems like a dream:

> The other night to bed I went,
> Was I really in Africa, or was it
> something I dreamt?
> Did I really have a holiday there?
> Can one have a dream other people can
> share?
> Did I really dream all that lovely sun?
> The good times we had, all that fun?
> That lovely warm weather, those
> gorgeous blue skies?
> No, I couldn't have dreamed those tearful
> goodbyes.
> In the morning I wake to find out it's
> true,
> I did spend a holiday out there with you.
> My souvenirs I see here and there dotted,
> An elephant, a crocodile, a dress navy
> blue-spotted.
> Memories flood back of the good times
> we had,
> Dreams do come true, things can't all be
> bad.

Memories will last though our suntans
fade,
Yes, we'll always remember the trip that
we made.

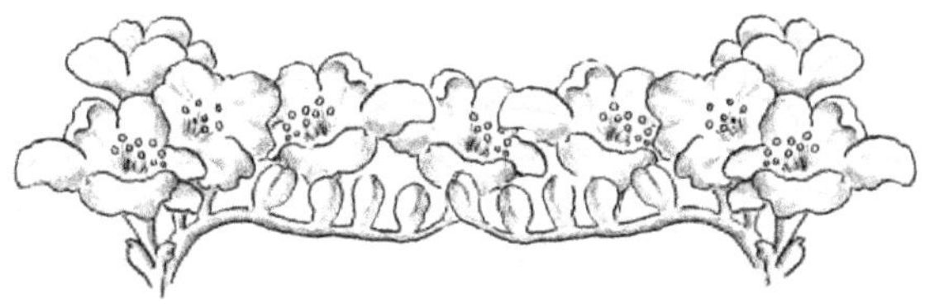

# Odds & Ends

## War Time Rations

4 oz bacon
8 oz sugar
2 oz tea
8 oz meat
2 oz cheese
2 oz butter
4 oz marge
2 oz cooking fat
1 egg a fortnight
2½ pints milk a week
12 oz sweets a month

## Jessie's Slippers

Knit 25 stitches till a square then cast off one stitch every row until there are five stitches left then sew up sides.

## For Arthritis

Light-coloured raisins, cover with gin and leave in open for seven days till all the gin evaporates, stirring once or twice. Cover raisins and eat nine raisins a day.

## Cheesecake

1 jelly
¼ pint of water (hot)
Cream and low-fat cheese
Digestive biscuits

- Make up jelly and add more water.
- Mix cream and low-fat cheese together.
- Mix jelly with biscuits and press into dish.
- Add cream and cheese and spread over biscuits and jelly.
- Freeze for ½ hour.

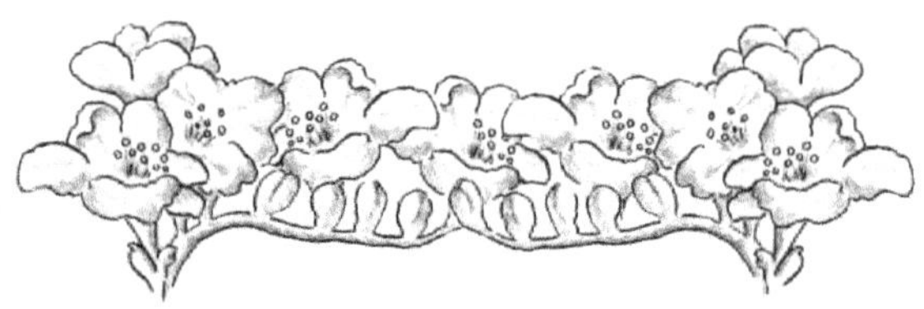

www.ingramcontent.com/pod-product-compliance
Lightning Source LLC
LaVergne TN
LVHW010941100826
845153LV00002B/111